# Praise for the Innovative Leadership Workbook for College Students

**This workbook provides a framework for innovative leadership—an approach our students are seeking and one our communities desperately need. It is an effective teaching tool for educators and a guide for any student who is seeking to develop as a citizen and leader.**

---

In an ideal world, a seasoned mentor will guide you through the early stages of your development as a leader. For those of you who lack that mentor, there's the *Innovative Leadership Workbook for College Students*. Guided by this book, you'll develop an understanding, testing, and learning about your own leadership.

*Jim Ritchie-Dunham, PhD, President of the Institute for Strategic Clarity and Adjunct Faculty, ITAM Business School, Harvard University*

◼◼◼◼◼◼

For our leaders, global competence and citizenship are indispensable qualifications for working cooperatively to seek and implement solutions to the significant challenges we currently face. *The Innovative Leadership Workbook for College Students* is a gift for students who are serious about learning leadership and having collaborative, productive interactions with people of international backgrounds. It is replete with tools, models, questions, processes, and reflections about the inner and outer work that's necessary to develop.

*William Brustein, PhD, Vice Provost for Global Strategies and International Affairs at the Ohio State University, winner of the 2014 Senator Paul Simon Award for Comprehensive Campus Internationalization*

◼◼◼◼◼◼

*Innovative Leadership for College Students* dissolves any stigma that leadership is only available to a chosen few. By focusing on innovative leadership, the authors empower students to focus on exploration and understanding of self and connectivity to a larger common good. In doing so, the authors provide us with a field manual for reasserting our commitment to graduating students who, by their example, will help to strengthen our communities.

*Drew Stelljes, PhD, Assistant Vice President for Student Engagement and Leadership at the College of William and Mary*

◼◼◼◼◼◼

In order for organizations to flourish in today's business, academic, and governmental environments it is critical that people work in groups. No longer can the lone individual perform all the functions necessary to compete successfully. As a result, we need more leaders who can coordinate the activities of many individuals in pursuit of a common goal. Developing the skills to be that kind of leader used to take years of experience, and keen observation of what works and what does not. But there is some urgency to train more leaders, more quickly. The lessons provided in this workbook can facilitate the training of leaders at younger ages. These lessons can help jumpstart the learning process, and provide a foundation upon which to begin the lifelong journey toward becoming a great leader.

*Susan Nittrouer, PhD, Professor and Chair, Department of Speech, Language, and Hearing Sciences, University of Florida*

◼◼◼◼◼◼

Preparing tomorrow's leaders for the global economy starts today...and in the classroom. This timely and efficient workbook delineates the core competencies that today's college students need for acquiring strong leadership skills. The workbook provides a roadmap of theory and practice to guide leadership development necessary for navigating the complexities of a constantly evolving global environment.

*Kelechi A. Kalu, PhD, Vice Provost for International Affairs and Professor of Political Science at University of California, Riverside*

As a student getting ready to start a professional career, it is essential to build a foundation of leadership skills during college. Learning to drive positive change through clarifying your personal values and beliefs is essential to developing as a leader. The *Innovative Leadership Workbook for College Students* will take you step-by-step through the process of establishing a solid and personal leadership foundation for future career success.

*Ryan Kucera, Student, the Ohio State University,*
*Mechanical Engineering*

■■■■■■

Strong technical skills are the foundation of a great engineer. Like engineers, the most successful leaders best augment their skills with self-awareness, authenticity, an ability to manage multiple highly complex issues, and an ability to navigate organizational politics with finesse. This workbook helps strong performers build on those skills to become stronger individual contributors and highly effective leaders.

*Ahmet Selamet PhD, Chair, Department of Mechanical*
*and Aerospace Engineering, the Ohio State University*

■■■■■■

In today's complex world, it is important to develop and practice leadership skills in college if one is to position new graduates for career success. Leadership evolves from leading self to leading student groups, to leading in more complex organizations. Learning to become the person that others willingly follow is a lifelong journey, and this workbook provides a terrific foundation to build upon.

*Susan Cannon, PhD, author of* The Way of The Mysterial Woman: Upgrading How You Live, Love, and Lead, *and Professor of Organizational Development and Leadership at Fielding Graduate University*

■■■■■■

This workbook encourages students to take initiative and become the authors of their own leadership journeys. It offers opportunities to utilize innovation for advancing leadership development and advocates for a vulnerable and individual process. The activities and assessments in the workbook could significantly impact the lives of students because it inspires them to look at their values and their vision and find alignment between the two. When creating my own compelling vision, I experienced dissonance important for my personal growth when the activity pushed me to see that my vision did not include my core value. I believe all college students should take advantage of this amazing book.

*Lisa Combs, Student, the Ohio State University, Political Science and English*

■■■■■■

As an administrator invested in college student leadership development, I recommend this highly experiential workbook to student leaders at all skill and experience levels. The authors pose genuine, supportive questions to spark critical thinking and introspection throughout the workbook, and then illuminate concepts through sample student responses to help ground the process in application. This guided self-reflection assists readers in understanding that leadership is a process and a lifelong journey of development; a crucial perspective, especially when working with others to turn a vision into reality.

*Brent Turner, MA, Executive Director, Campus Life, Northwestern University*

■■■■■■

Leading self and leading others are intimately intertwined. Authors Maureen Metcalf and Amy Barnes provide a comprehensive, practical approach for developing the foundation to become a great leader of both self and others. The workbook walks the reader through a series of exercises and reflection questions designed to increase awareness and support action. Case studies of three students offer a broad range of examples that are easy to relate to.

*Ryan Forrey, PharmD, MS, Director of Pharmacy, Emory University Hospital Midtown*

# INNOVATIVE LEADERSHIP WORKBOOK

## FOR COLLEGE STUDENTS

Field Tested Processes and Worksheets for
Developing Innovative Leadership

MAUREEN METCALF, MBA
AMY BARNES, MA, EDD

FOREWORD BY PAUL PRYZ

First Published by
Integral Publishers
1418 N. Jefferson Ave.
Tucson, AZ 85712

Published in the United States with printing and
distribution in the United Kingdom, Australia, and
the European Union.

ISBN: 978-1-4951-5917-6

First Printing December 2015

Cover Design, Graphics and Layout by
Creative Spot - www.creativespot.com

# Acknowledgments

This book represents the synthesis of the primary authors' twenty-five years of research, work experience, and consulting. It integrates best practices from university teaching as well as corporate leadership development programs, an active coaching practice, and input from our interns. We would first like to acknowledge our employers and colleagues for providing practical opportunities to teach and learn and build strong skills in college student development among many others. It was this solid foundation that allowed us to create this methodology and apply it to college students.

As a theoretical foundation, we worked with or studied the work of many thought leaders in the fields of leadership development, developmental psychology, integral theory, college student development, and others. The theoretical giants on whose hard work we built the Innovative Leadership and Organizational Transformation models include: Susanne Cook-Greuter, PhD, Belinda Gore, PhD, Hilke Richmer, EdD, Roxanne Howe-Murphy, EdD, Susan Komives, EdD, John Dugan, PhD, Julie Owen, PhD, Ken Wilber and Terri O'Fallon, PhD. Several of these leaders shared not only their theories, but also ongoing guidance and encouragement, helping to create a solid framework that is comprehensive and theoretically grounded—and, for that, we are grateful.

Other contributors who helped to make this book a reality:

Belinda Gore, PhD, Jiaqi Guo (Kelly), Anthony C. Calabrese, Shelby Bradford, Eric Philippou, Derek Colston, and Luke Moore.

Friends, mentors, and colleagues who served as constant cheerleaders and readers, made suggestions, listened to stories and dreams about the book, and helped make it come to fruition; the teachers, trainers, and mentors who taught how to lead with authenticity and integrity.

Students of the Ohio State University and Capital University who participated as case studies for this book or provided feedback, as well as Capital University MBA students who gave feedback on the book by virtue of doing graduate work using the field book.

Family who provided continual support and encouragement as well as inspiring us to be thoughtful, dedicated to work, and to contribute to the world in a meaningful way, especially, Pete, Sophia, Luke, Bob and Rae, Jan, and Jessica.

Publisher and friend, Russ Volckmann, PhD.

Graphic design and layout firm Creative Spot, development editor Sara Phelps, as well as editors, reviewers, endorsers, thought partners, and countless others who spent untold hours making this possible.

# Table of Contents

# FOREWORD

This quote by Warren Bennis, widely known as a leadership author and leader in higher education, is my favorite. Hands down. It is simple, eloquent, easy to remember. And right. Clearly, this is my opinion, but as someone who has read and heard numerous quotes on leadership throughout my life, I keep coming back to this.

We have many choices to make in our lives. We can choose our career, our partner, our attitude, our dinner option, but perhaps there is no more important choice to make in our lives than how we are going to make a difference with the limited time we have on this planet. Far too many of us choose to live lives of insignificance and mediocrity because we don't see ourselves as leaders, or as even having the capability to make a difference in our communities—much less our own lives. So we bounce from day to day without purpose or passion.

I have used this quote from Bennis quite often in my work leading a not-for-profit organization in an attempt to de-mystify the concept of leading. In attempts to define it, we have made leading far too complicated. I have been keeping a list of all the books on leadership that have thrown another adjective in front of "leadership" to sell their version of it. Ultimate leadership. Super leadership. Principled leadership. My favorites being liquid leadership, food leadership (seriously), and boot strap leadership. Go ahead, look them up on Amazon or in the bookstore. They are there.

A good question to ask is, "Why are there so many books out there on leadership?" Other than because it is a popular topic and people want to make money by window dressing their own version of leadership, I can think of only one other connected reason: People want to understand leadership. They want to see how it's defined and how to "do" it. So, they buy the books.

We need leaders. We need them now more than ever. We long to be led. Really led. I don't care about the number of followers that a leader has as much as I want to see people using their lives to pursue something that they are passionate about and that will make the world a better place in a small (or large) way. People who have made a choice to do so.

All of this brings me to this book. I am passionate about helping young people connect with the idea that they can lead. Not because they have a title next to their names, but because they have a passion, skill, or talent that the world needs, and they just haven't realized it yet. That is where the concept of building leadership skills while in college comes into play.

We need to do more to help young people, in particular, emerge as leaders and figure out that they can lead and know that we need them to lead. They don't have to be in front of the room, but they need to participate in the room. They don't need the title, but they need to act like they have it. They don't need followers, but they need to do something that is worth following. They need the patience to plant seeds, try new ideas, and fail miserably. Student leaders need our support, our encouragement, and our willingness to set them loose and figure it out on their own. We cannot weigh them down with the ideas of the past and how past generations saw leadership. They need to make their own meaning of the concept and wrestle in the mud with hard conversations that produce hard solutions. They need us to get out of their way and give them room to grow with their own understanding and vision. They need a guide, not a prescription.

Maureen and Amy have done an excellent job of providing the questions, but not the answers. They have cut through the complexity of the topic and framed the process of becoming a leader in a way that is simple, but not easy. The activities and conversations in this workbook can only help readers figure out where they can best make a difference, and, more importantly, what they need to do to make a difference.

Jim Collins said that the enemy of great is being good, and that is precisely why we have so few things and institutions that are truly great. We need to push, we need to engage, and we need to help others realize that they, too, have the capability and the capacity to lead.

And then we can only hope that you choose to lead.

Enjoy the journey.


*Paul Pyrz*
*President, LeaderShape*

# INTRODUCTION
# INNOVATIVE LEADERSHIP FOR COLLEGE STUDENTS

Of all the topics surrounding leadership today, innovation is one of the most significant. Yet despite the volume of resources exploring both innovation and leadership, most approaches provide directional solutions that are merely anecdotal. In addition, these fictive solutions lack sufficient information for leaders to utilize their own capacities to make measurable change. As a college student, you are provided with many opportunities to develop your own leadership skills and capacities through coursework, co-curricular involvement, and part or full-time work experiences. You are the future leaders of our companies, our nonprofit organizations, our government, and our education system. It is extremely important that we, as a society, invest in the development of our future leaders. We know that leadership plays a critical role in today's ever changing world, and that innovation is a strategic necessity for tackling the tough problems we face today and those we will face in the near future.

Still, ensuing questions on how to lead and where to innovate remain puzzling for leaders and world leaders: What is the role of leadership in times of looming uncertainty? How will organizations innovate to overcome largely unprecedented challenges? And how can we work together and leverage our strengths to more effectively address the future small and large challenges we will encounter in our organizations?

This workbook is designed to help answer those questions and to help you with the critical self-evaluation needed to refine and innovate your own leadership skills. It is fundamentally about leadership, yet equally an account of applying innovation.

Many students take a passive approach to leadership during college. It is as though they are waiting to become a leader... someday. The truth is that we need you to be leaders now. Today. Not tomorrow or three years from now. You can begin developing leadership competencies and personal awareness now, as a student—and, if you do, you will have a distinct advantage in the workplace when you graduate. Figuring out now who you are, what you value, and how to tap into your innovative self will enhance your experience as a leader later.

Leading within the culture of a college campus is a great place to test approaches to leadership and management that will translate to the real world. If you haven't done so already, sign up for a student organization or an intramural sport, or volunteer for a local nonprofit. You can gain experience as a leader when you volunteer for leadership positions in which you will be given responsibility or oversight of a team. Internships and part-time jobs are also great ways to get hands-on leadership experience. By putting yourself in these environments and through the lessons from this workbook, you will gain invaluable knowledge and skills for the workplace. You will also be able to develop your empathy as a leader by examining team situations from not only your perspective, but from the perspective of others around you. Leadership empathy and the ability to inspire cultural alignment, along with other important leadership activities, make a significant impact on any organization and must be implemented as shrewdly as is strategic planning.

This workbook explores a number of approaches to elaborate on both your personal development as a leader and your innovative abilities by providing exercises designed to create space for you to grow and learn. Both becoming a better leader and optimizing innovation hinge on your ability to authentically examine your own inner makeup which, in turn, will allow you to make real change.

At the same time, you must actively address some limitations. Despite their collective value, many conventional applications of leadership and innovation have proven elusive and even problematic in real-world scenarios. For example, consider a work environment or a student organization that you have been involved with in the past few years, one that emphasized innovating programs, processes, and productivity. Productivity and program improvements are undoubtedly critical, but how organization members make sense of their experience is equally vital to team engagement and commitment. Innovating products and improving functionality without also creating a better team environment or a more supportive organizational culture, often appears to pay off in the short term, yet the imbalanced focus produces lopsided decision-making and shortsighted leadership that has lasting adverse consequences.

Learning to combine leadership with innovation requires you to transform the way you perceive yourself, others, and the contexts within which you lead. By vigorously looking at your own experience, including motivations, inclinations, interpersonal skills, and proficiencies, you can optimize your effectiveness. Through deep examination and reflection, you learn to balance the skills you will and have acquired, all the while setting the stage for further growth. In essence, you discover how to strategically and tactically innovate your own leadership the same way you innovate in other aspects of your organizations and the contexts from which you navigate your world.

## Marrying Innovation and Leadership

Where do you lead? We discussed some contexts in which a college student might lead, but leadership is more expansive than just formal leadership roles. If you are a member of a community (your residence hall or in your apartment), a participant in a group project for class, or even as a part of a class discussion, then you have the opportunity to be a leader. However, are you tapping into your talents and abilities to be a leader in these contexts? Do you know how to lead, or develop your leadership skills, within these different contexts? Leadership needs innovation the way innovation demands leadership, and, by marrying the two, you can improve your capacity for growth and improved effectiveness.

**What does innovating leadership really mean?** Let's explore innovating leadership in a more tangible way by defining it in practical terms, and moving beyond the conventional meaning of each term. For example, most definitions of "leadership" are almost exclusively fashioned around emulating certain kinds of behaviors: leader X did "this" to achieve success, and leader Y did "that" to enhance organizational performance.

While initially useful, such approaches are essentially formulas for *imitating leadership*, and, therefore, are likely ineffectual over the long term. This is common among college students in leadership roles. They look around and watch other leaders, then try to imitate those behaviors. Skills can certainly be learned by observing and then practicing them, but it is important to understand that you need to develop a unique and effective way of leading using your *own* strengths and talents. This book will help you discover the unique ways to be an innovative leader rather than copying a leadership style that you have observed in someone else. Innovating leadership cannot be applied as a monolithic theory, or as simple prescriptive guidance. It must take place through your own intelligence and stem from your own unique sensibilities.

Have you ever felt like an imposter within a group in which you were given responsibilities that you thought were beyond your capabilities? There is actually a psychological term for this called "imposter syndrome," and at one time or another, most of us have felt that way. Many young leaders experience this either in college or at the early stages in their career when they don't yet feel "qualified" to do the work they are being asked to do. Every new leader feels these same feelings of fear and inadequacy, or at least they should. These feelings help us to ground ourselves, and dig a bit deeper to discover our own unique characteristics to make us the best leaders we can be. Understanding yourself both individually and within a group context is the best way to tackle these feelings of inadequacy and build the confidence you will need to do the job well.

In order to enhance this self-awareness process, you will need a foundational basis from which to explore both leadership and innovation.

Let's start by straightforwardly defining leadership:

> **Leadership is the ability to effect change for the betterment of others and the greater community by clarifying personal values, beliefs and intentions, aligning those beliefs with actions, and by positively influencing organizational culture and systems.**

Within this context, leadership involves a two-fold ***process of influence***: *strategic* influence to inspire vision and direction, and *tactical* influence to guide functional execution.

Leadership influences individual intentions and cultural norms by inspiring purpose and alignment. It equally influences an individual's actions and organizational efficiencies through tactical decisions.

Innovation, as an extension of leadership, refers to the novel ways in which we advance that influence across the four elements of personal values, beliefs and intentions, personal actions, organizational beliefs (culture) and organizational systems. We will discuss each of these elements in much greater detail in the section on situational analysis.

Innovation is a novel advancement that influences organizations: personally, behaviorally, culturally, and systematically.

Notice that in addition to linking the relationship of leadership to innovation, we're also relating to them as an essential part of our individual experience. Just as with leadership and innovation, the way you uniquely experience and influence the world is defined through a mutual interplay of *personal, behavioral, cultural*, and *systematic* events. These same core dimensions that ground leadership and innovation, also provide a context and mirror for *your total experience* in any given moment or on any given occasion.

This is best understood through an example from Maureen:

> "When I began teaching an innovative leadership class teaching to a new audience for this material—a group of undergraduate engineers—I knew I needed to demonstrate strong leadership and ensure that I was being personally innovative. I needed to evaluate my *beliefs* about this project and ask if I was willing to think differently.
>
> Next, I needed to think about *behaviors*—how I behaved and how I would ask them to behave. Was I willing to try different behaviors even if they felt awkward and uncomfortable? Since this was an engineering class I needed to pay attention to how they saw the world (*organization*) and make an effort to understand what they valued. Many saw engineering expertise as the most important skill to possess, yet as a group they valued openness, learning, and having a caring instructor.
>
> Finally, I needed to consider the *systems*. As a faculty member I was teaching a class, but how would this innovative experiment be different? Could we have class outside the classroom? Since the activities would be qualitative, rather than quantitative, how would I grade their assignments? Was there a different approach that fit within the school's requirements, but still allowed us as a group to have the best possible experience? So, in order to truly innovate, I needed to be willing to examine myself and the organization, and take action based on a solid understanding of the factors that would influence my success and our success."

Optimally then, leadership is influencing through an explicit balance of these core dimensions. Innovation naturally follows as a creative advancement of this basic alignment. Marrying leadership with innovation allows you both to ground and articulate in a way that can create a context for dynamic personal development—a process that we will help you navigate throughout this book.

> **Innovating leadership means leaders influence by *equally* engaging their personal intention and action with the organization's culture and systems.**

Though we are, in a sense, defining innovative leadership very broadly, we are also making a distinct point. We are saying that the core aspects that comprise your experience—whether personal intention, action, cultural, or systematic—are inextricably interconnected. If you affect one, you affect them all.

So, if, for example, you implement a strategy to realign a student organization's value system over the next two years, you will also affect personal motivations (intentions), behavioral outcomes and organizational culture. To deny the mutual interplay of any one of the four dimensions misses the full picture. You can only innovate leadership by addressing reality in a comprehensive fashion.

Leadership innovation happens naturally, but can be accelerated through the use of a structured process involving self-exploration, allowing you to authentically enhance your leadership beyond simply following procedures and task execution.

Many student leaders today focus entirely on accomplishments: What tasks did I get done today? We often think that if we are busy with responsibilities and tasks, then we are leading. Completing tasks or guiding projects is certainly one aspect of leading but it is not the full picture. Without the strategy to create a vision or the personal awareness to enhance communication in the group, then the emphasis on the people in the group gets lost among the tasks and the leader is less effective. An innovative approach to leadership ensures that all aspects of a process are simultaneously being addressed and an innovative leader makes sure to consider their leadership impact on the individuals, community, and culture in the organization.

To summarize, leadership innovation is the process of self-improvement and increased self-awareness within the context of organizations thus allowing successful leadership to raise the bar on performance without losing sight of the people and culture of the organization.

An innovative leader is defined as someone who consistently delivers results using:

- **Strategic leadership** that inspires individual intentions and *goals* and organizational *vision and culture*;

- **Task leadership** that influences an individual's *actions* and the organization's *systems and processes*; and,

- **Holistic leadership** that aligns all core dimensions: *individual intention and action, along with organizational culture and systems.*

## The Opportunity of Innovative Leadership

The overwhelming focus of today's organizational changes is on system functionality and efficiency. Any person who has interacted with organizations or companies today as a customer is aware of this emphasis and has likely experienced what happens when an organization places efficiency or functionality over the importance of personal connection. Though necessary, functionality and efficiency are only *part* of the total picture.

Being guided by more strategically inclusive decisions may be the difference between managing failure and creating tangible success. Your leadership must consider a more balanced definition of innovation that comprehensively aligns vision, teams, and systems, and integrates the perspectives of the people serving, or those being served, in the overall focus of your impact.

This balanced approach to leadership and innovation is transformative for both you and the groups you are a part of, and can help you to respond more effectively to challenges within and outside organizations. Innovating your leadership gives you the means to adapt in ways that allow optimal performance, even within an organizational climate fraught with continual change and complexity.

Student organizations, sport teams, and service organizations on campuses are surprisingly change-oriented because of the annual nature of the leadership turnover. Often, the time that a leader has to positively influence an organization is as short as nine or ten months (one academic year). This is a great training ground for your future as a leader in the work world. If you can learn to function successfully in an ever-changing organizational leadership scenario while also considering the needs of the individuals on your team, then you are building important skills for the future. And an innovative leadership approach gives you the capacity to openly recognize and critically examine aspects of yourself, as well as your organization's culture and systems, in the midst of any change or challenge that you may experience.

## Defining What an Innovative Leader Does

What are specific behaviors that differentiate an innovative leader from a traditional leader? In this time of rapid change, a successful innovative leader is one who can consistently:

- Clarify and effectively articulate vision

- Develop greater self-understanding and influence the development of other leaders

- Build effective teams by helping peers and colleagues engage their own leadership strengths

- Cultivate alliances and partnerships

- Anticipate and aggressively respond to both challenges and opportunities

- Develop robust and resilient solutions

- Develop and test hypotheses like a scientist– scientists learn from their experiments rather than fearing failure

- Measure, learn, and refine on an ongoing basis


To further illustrate some of the qualities of innovative leadership, we offer this comparison between traditional leadership and innovative leadership:

| TRADITIONAL LEADERSHIP | INNOVATIVE LEADERSHIP |
|---|---|
| Leader is guided primarily by desire for personal success and peripherally by organizational success. | Leader is humbly guided by a more altruistic vision of success based on both performance and the positive impact the organization can make. |
| Leadership decision style is "command and control;" leader has all the answers. | Leader leverages team for answers as part of the decision-making process. |
| Leader picks a direction in "black/white" manner; tends to dogmatically stay the course. | Leader perceives and behaves like a scientist: continually experimenting, measuring, and testing for improvement and exploring new models and approaches. |
| Leader focuses on being technically correct and in charge. | Leader is continually learning and developing self and others; leader admits mistakes and sees them as an opportunity for growth, expresses learning gained, and makes improvements/ amends based on that learning and growth |
| Leader manages people to perform by being autocratic and controlling. | Leader motivates people to perform through strategic focus, mentoring and coaching, an emphasis on personal strengths, and interpersonal intelligence. |
| Leader tends to the numbers and primarily utilizes quantitative measures that drive those numbers. | Leader tends to financial performance, employee engagement, community impact, and cultural cohesion while qualitatively evaluating the collective impact of the work being done. |

## Getting the Most from the Workbook

Before you get started, take a moment to think about why you purchased this workbook. Setting goals and understanding your intentions and expectations about the exercises will help you focus on identifying and driving your desired results.

In order to help clarify, consider the following questions:

- What are the five to seven events and choices that brought you to where you are today?

- How did these events and choices contribute to choosing to buy and use this workbook? (or, if you are using this book for a class, how did these events and choices contribute to you choosing to enroll in the class?)

- What stands out in the list you have made? Are there any surprises or patterns?

- What do you hope to gain from your investment in leadership development?

- What meaningful impact will it produce in your leadership experiences now as well as in your professional career and personal life?

In addition to your reflection on the above questions, here are some ideas we recommend to help you get the most out of this experience. It is our observation that people who adhere to the following agreements tend to have a deeper and more enriching overall experience. By participating in this fashion, you will generate a richer evaluation of yourself and most effectively take advantage of what this workbook has to offer.

Take a moment to reflect on these guidelines:

| AGREEMENT | RELATED ACTION OR BEHAVIOR |
|---|---|
| 1. Be fully present | Let go of thoughts about other activities while you read. Bring your full attention to the work |
| 2. Take responsibility for your own success | Be 100% responsible for the outcome of your engagement with this material |
| 3. Participate as fully as possible | Complete all the exercises to the best of your abilities. Apply the concepts and skills that work best for you, and modify those that do not |
| 4. Practice good life management | Invest time at scheduled intervals to work on the materials when you are mentally and emotionally at your best |
| 5. Lean into optimal discomfort; take risks without overwhelming yourself | Be candid, open, and direct. Allow yourself to be curious and vulnerable |
| 6. Take the process seriously, and more importantly take yourself lightly. Make this a positive and rewarding experience | Allow yourself balance. Find the lesson and humor in both your successes and mistakes. Most importantly, have fun! |

## How to Use the Workbook

After this introduction to innovative leadership, each chapter builds on a series of exercises and reflection questions designed to guide you through the process of developing your own abilities as an innovative leader. We recommend that you use the following sequence to help efficiently process the material:

### 1. Read Intently

Read the chapter through completely, as we introduce and illustrate an integrated set of concepts for each element in building innovative leadership.

### 2. Contemplate

Using a set of carefully chosen applications and specifically designed exercises will help you to embody the work and bring the concepts to life. Through a process of dynamic examination and reflection, you will be encouraged to contemplate some significant, real-life implications of change. Many of the exercises can be done on your own; others are designed to be conducted with input from your family, friends, co-workers, and fellow student leaders.

### 3. Link Your Experiences

As you sequentially build your understanding, you will begin noticing habits and conditioned patterns that present you with clear opportunities for growth. Though you may encounter personal resistance along the way, you will also discover new and exciting strengths. As you become more adept at using these ideas, you will find yourself increasingly capable of proactive engagement with the concepts, along with an ability to respond to situations requiring innovative leadership with greater capacity.

Once you have completed the process, you will have created a plan to grow as an innovative leader. Ultimately, implementing that plan will be up to you and your team.

# ASSESSMENT

## Innovative Leadership for Emerging Leaders

Leadership Behaviors

Situational Analysis

Resilience

Leadership Maturity

Leader Type

The following is a short self-assessment to help you identify your own scores relating to Innovative Leadership for university students. It is organized by the five domains of Innovative Leadership, and will give you a general sense of where you want to focus your efforts. We encourage you to take this survey as a way to get a snapshot of where you excel and where you may want to focus your energies. Think about the last year when determining your answer. If you are not sure, select "3" as the survey will not score properly unless each question is answered. The survey should take about 10 minutes to complete.

### Assessment Instructions:

- Complete the 7–9 questions per page. Each of the five sections will appear on a separate page.

- Complete each page and calculate your score on each of the five elements of innovative leadership.

# Score Yourself on Awareness of Leader Type and Self-Management

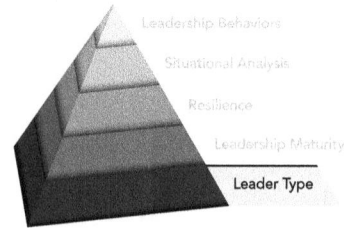

Think about how you responded to work situations in the past year and answer the following questions using this scale:

*Never (1)    Rarely (2)    Sometimes (3)    Often (4)    Almost always (5)*

1.  I use the insight from this assessment to understand my type. Specifically, I understand my gifts and limitations, and try to leverage my strengths and manage my limitations.    **1 2 3 4 5**

2.  I have a reflection practice where I understand, actively monitor, and work with my "fixations" (negative thought patterns).    **1 2 3 4 5**

3.  I have a clear sense of who I am and what I want to contribute to the world.    **1 2 3 4 5**

4.  I manage my emotional reactions to allow me to respond with socially appropriate behavior.    **1 2 3 4 5**

5.  I am aware of what causes me stress and actively manage it.    **1 2 3 4 5**

6.  I have positive coping strategies.    **1 2 3 4 5**

7.  I actively seek ways to feel empowered even when the organization may not.    **1 2 3 4 5**

---

**Total Score**

-  If your overall score in this category is 24 or less, it's time to pay attention to your leadership type and self-management.

-  If your overall score in this category is 25 to 31, you are in the healthy range, but could still benefit from some focus on your leadership type and self-management.

-  If your overall score is 32 or above, Congratulations! You are self-aware and using your leadership type to increase your effectiveness.

# Score Yourself on Developmental Perspective Aligned with Innovation

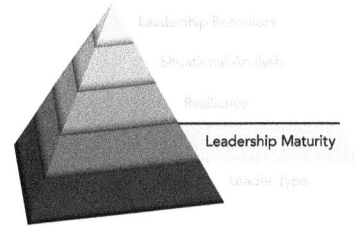

Think about how you responded to work situations over the past year and answer the following questions using this scale:

*Never (1)    Rarely (2)    Sometimes (3)    Often (4)    Almost always (5)*

1.  I have a sense of life purpose and do work that is generally aligned with that purpose.                                    1 2 3 4 5

2.  I am motivated by the impact I make on the world more than on personal notoriety.                                          1 2 3 4 5

3.  I try to live my life according to my personal values.                                                                    1 2 3 4 5

4.  I believe that collaboration across groups is important to accomplish our goals.                                          1 2 3 4 5

5.  I believe that getting results must be balanced with treating people fairly and kindly.                                    1 2 3 4 5

6.  I consistently seek input from others to test my thinking and expand my perspective.                                       1 2 3 4 5

7.  I think about the impact of my activities on our community and beyond.                                                     1 2 3 4 5

8.  I am open and curious, always trying new things and learning from all of them.                                            1 2 3 4 5

9.  I appreciate the value of rules and am willing to question them in a professional manner.                                  1 2 3 4 5

## Total Score

- If your overall score in this category is 27 or less, it's time to pay attention to your developmental level including testing your current level and focusing on developing in the area of developmental perspectives.

- If your overall score in this category is 28 to 35, you are in the healthy range, but could still benefit from some focus on developing in the area of developmental perspectives.

- If your score is 36 or above, Congratulations! Your developmental level appears to be aligned with innovate leadership, yet this assessment is only a subset of a full assessment.

# Score Yourself on Resilience

Think about how you responded to work situations in the past year and answer the following questions using this scale:

*Never (1)    Rarely (2)    Sometimes (3)    Often (4)    Almost always (5)*

1.  I consistently take care of my physical needs, such as getting enough sleep and exercise.          **1  2  3  4  5**

2.  I have a sense of purpose and get to do activities that contribute to that purpose daily.          **1  2  3  4  5**

3.  I have a high degree of self-awareness and manage my thoughts actively.          **1  2  3  4  5**

4.  I have a strong support system consisting of a healthy mix of friends, colleagues, and family.          **1  2  3  4  5**

5.  I can reframe challenges to find something of value in most situations.          **1  2  3  4  5**

6.  I build strong trusting relationships at work.          **1  2  3  4  5**

7.  I am aware of my own "self-talk" and actively manage it.          **1  2  3  4  5**

8.  I have a professional development plan that includes gaining skills and additional perspectives.          **1  2  3  4  5**

---

## Total Score

- If your overall score in this category is 24 or less, it's time to pay attention to your resilience.

- If your overall score in this category is 25 to 31, you are in the healthy range, but could still benefit from some focus on resilience.

- If your score is 32 or above, congratulations! You are likely performing well in the area of resilience, yet this assessment is only a subset of the full resilience assessment.

# Score Yourself on Managing Alignment of Self and Groups

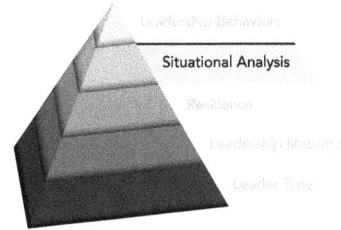

Think about how you responded to work situations over the past year and answer the following questions using this scale:

*Never (1)    Rarely (2)    Sometimes (3)    Often (4)    Almost always (5)*

1.  I am aware of my own passions and values.    **1 2 3 4 5**

2.  My behavior consistently reflects my goals and values.    **1 2 3 4 5**

3.  I feel safe pushing back when I am asked to do things that are not aligned with my values.    **1 2 3 4 5**

4.  I am aware that my behavior and decisions as a leader have an impact on the people I work with (or people in my classes).    **1 2 3 4 5**

5.  I am deliberate about aligning my behaviors with the behaviors the group values and I pay attention to delivering the desired results (group could be classes, clubs, or roommates in addition to work).    **1 2 3 4 5**

6.  I am aware of how my values align with those of the organization and where they are misaligned; if there are misalignments, I try to find constructive ways address these differences.    **1 2 3 4 5**

---

**Total Score**

- If your overall score in this category is 18 or less, it's time to pay attention to your alignment with the group and also the alignment of culture and systems within the group that you are able to impact.

- If your overall score in this category is 19 to 23, you are in the healthy range, but could still benefit from some focus on alignment.

- If your score is 24 or above, congratulations! You are well aligned with the group, and the group's culture and systems are well-aligned.

# Score Yourself on Leadership Behaviors

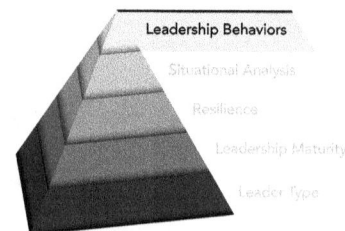

Think about how you responded to work situations over the past year and answer the following questions using this scale:

*Never (1)     Rarely (2)     Sometimes (3)     Often (4)     Almost always (5)*

1. I tend to be proactive—I anticipate what is coming next and actively manage it. (*This may be primarily in my personal life.*)          **1 2 3 4 5**

2. I focus on creating results in a way that helps me grow and develop along with those who work for me while accomplishing our tasks.          **1 2 3 4 5**

3. I think about the impact of my actions on the group rather than just getting the job done.          **1 2 3 4 5**

4. I see how my work contributes to group success.          **1 2 3 4 5**

5. I deliberately try to improve myself and the group.          **1 2 3 4 5**

6. I take time to mentor others, even when I am busy (this could be formal or informal mentoring).          **1 2 3 4 5**

7. I consider myself a personal learner because of the time I spend reading and trying new ideas and activities. I am curious.          **1 2 3 4 5**

8. I have the courage to speak out in a professional manner when asked to do something with which I disagree.          **1 2 3 4 5**

9. I accomplish results by working with and through others in a positive and constructive manner.          **1 2 3 4 5**

---

**Total Score**

- If your overall score in this category is 27 or less, it's time to pay attention to your alignment with the group and also the alignment of culture and systems within the group that you are able to impact.

- If your overall score in this category is 28 to 35, you are in the healthy range, but could still benefit from some focus on alignment.

- If your score is 36 or above, congratulations! You are well aligned with the group, and the group's culture and systems are well-aligned.

# CHAPTER 1

## Elements of Innovative Leadership

Chapter 1 begins with a discussion of innovative leadership and provides the general framework for innovating how you lead. Innovative leadership comprises the five elements presented and discussed in this chapter; then, these elements are then applied throughout chapters two through seven and explain how you can become an innovative leader.

### Fig. 1.1 Five Elements of Innovative Leadership

What is truly unique in this approach to leadership is the broad scope of the model that comprises the five elements. Theorists have looked at each of these individual elements for years and have suggested that mastering one or two is typically sufficient for effective leaders. We believe in a less complex world that this may have been true, but it is no longer the case. As the twenty-first century unfolds, the most effective leaders will need a more holistic view than at any other time in history. In this chapter we will define and describe the individual elements of innovative leadership and think about how they interact.

Up until now, much of your identity was influenced greatly by family and peers. You may not have even thought about yourself outside the context of these important people or influences in your life. Self-understanding and self-awareness allow you to expand your perspective and build greater understanding of others. This capacity can be developed if you focus on your inner self as part of leadership development. The changes you experience between high school and college can accelerate your process of self-awareness, and your college years are a critical time to develop this greater self-awareness.

As a student leader, you have the opportunity to "test the waters" of leadership through involvement in student organizations and group projects in classes, even planning social outings with your friends is an opportunity to lead. Undoubtedly you have discovered that your approach to planning and communication in a group setting is not always the same as those around you. That is why it is so important to gain a greater understanding of your natural tendencies. Self-awareness will allow you to regulate your own behavior in a group and to be more understanding of the approaches of others. Part of the challenge in building innovative leadership is learning to leverage the clarity of your introspection. Looking inside yourself and examining how you behave around other people enables you to function in a highly grounded way, rather than operating from innate personal biases.

Leadership Behaviors

Situational Analysis

Resilience

Leadership Maturity

Leader Type

## Leader Type

When thinking about leadership, start by simply considering your disposition, tendencies, inclinations, and ways of thinking and acting. Innovating leadership hinges on understanding the manner in which you live your life. One way to observe this is by examining aspects of your inner being, often called Leader Type. The Leader Personality Type (or Leader Type) critically influences who you are as a leader. It is an essential foundation of your personal makeup and greatly shapes your leadership effectiveness. The ancient adage of "know thyself," holds true as a crucial underpinning in leadership performance.

It is important to keep in mind that this particular notion of type is something that is native to your being and generally does not change significantly over the course of your life. This is an essential point: By understanding your type and the types of others, you can begin to see situations without the bias of your own perceptions. You will have clearer understanding and will make more informed decisions with less speculation. You will learn to deeply understand the inner movements of your strengths, weaknesses, and core patterns. Leadership typing tools are helpful in promoting this kind of self-knowledge and pattern recognition.

> *By learning about these patterns, you can gain perspective on your life and start connecting the dots among your different experiences. Most of us have a concept about how we behave, but that idea is likely clouded and not entirely true. One of the hardest things for most people is to see themselves accurately. How astonishing it is to see through the clouds and recognize yourself clearly.*
>
> —Roxanne Howe-Murphy, *Deep Living*

Learning at this deeper level from your own inner dynamics can offer remarkable insight into areas of your life that, in your own personal experience, you may either exaggerate or under emphasize.

If you are part of an intact team such as a student organization, ask each team member to participate in the same assessment tool and to reflect both individually and as a group on the results. If you are reading this book without a group context to consider, taking what you learn into your next group setting and recognizing the different types of leaders sitting around the table with you will also make a positive difference.

## Leadership Maturity

In this workbook we explore developmental levels and perspectives as core elements in developing innovative leadership. Leadership Maturity significantly influences how you view your role in a group or the workplace, how you interact with other people, and how you solve problems. The term Leadership Maturity, can be described as "meaning making," that is, how you make meaning or sense of experiences. This is important because the algorithm you use to make sense of the world influences your thoughts and actions. Incorporating these perspectives is critical to developing innovative leadership.

In order to connect Leadership Maturity with Leader Type, let's look at how these models come together. Leadership research strongly suggests that although inherent Leader Type determines your tendency to lead, good leaders develop over time. While Leader Type is usually a constant over your lifetime, you have the capacity to grow and develop your Leadership Maturity. Therefore, it is often the case that leaders are perhaps both born *and* made. Type remains consistent during your life while developmental perspective is grown. This is an important differentiator in leadership effectiveness that allows you to see what can be changed and what should be accepted as innate personality type.

As a reference for Leadership Maturity, the stages outlined in the Leadership Identity Development (LID) Model (Komives et al., 2006) incorporate not just leadership growth for young adults, but the unique experiences that college students encounter in student organizations, sports teams, or class projects. The model identifies six stages of leader development: 1) Awareness, 2) Exploration/ Engagement, 3) Leader Identified, 4) Leader Differentiated, 5) Generativity, and 6) Integration/ Synthesis. The focus of LID is on moving leaders from dependency on others in the early stages to interdependency in later stages, from reliance on adults and older peers to self-efficacy. Role models are important, but at stage four students realize their own leadership capacities and identify the unique qualities and strengths of others. This creates greater appreciation of team members' contributions, encourages delegation and trust, and increases the capacity to process personal mistakes.

Another component is the "key transition" where students view leadership less as positional and more as a process. In early stages, one believes that a leader must hold a formal position (president, vice president, social chair). It can be a tough lesson for anyone to realize that a title doesn't necessarily indicate leadership, control, or the degree of control. Leadership occurs at all levels of an organization and even in unstructured environments where positions do not exist. In his popular TED talk "Everyday Leadership," Drew Dudley describes how we tend to define leadership as the very broad ability to change the world someday and lose sight of the smaller and incremental steps that it takes for huge changes to come about in the moments:

*...I worry sometimes that we spend so much time celebrating amazing things that hardly anybody can do that we've convinced ourselves that those are the only things worth celebrating, and we start to devalue the things that we can do every day, and we start to take moments where we truly are a leader and we don't let ourselves take credit for it, and we don't let ourselves feel good about it.*

—Drew Dudley

This quote illustrates the need for college students to embrace leadership in everyday actions and situations. It also supports the idea that peer mentorship can be leadership, just as students in later stages of the LID model mentor younger or less experienced leaders to generate long-term success for their organization or group. Students who advance to the last stages of the model view their leadership development as a never-ending process and continually seek new challenges and new perspectives.

What does this mean for you as a college student leader? We recommend that you challenge yourself to move through these important developmental stages. Research around college student leadership indicates that students' leadership development is enhanced through mentoring relationships, interactions, and meaningful conversations around socio-cultural issues, and involvement or service in the community (Dugan et al., 2012). It is easy to focus only on what is happening with classes and student organizations and to miss opportunities for engagement within the local community. To build your leadership level, consider ways to get involved in your community and challenge yourself to learn new perspectives from the diverse array of students, faculty, and staff that live and work around your school.

To learn about leadership as a process, become an active member and observe the non-positional leadership occurring around your organization. To move toward interdependency as a leader and build your own self-efficacy for leadership, take on new responsibilities, learn to share power, and encourage leadership at all levels of your organization. Your focus can also be on learning new skills and gaining greater self-awareness.

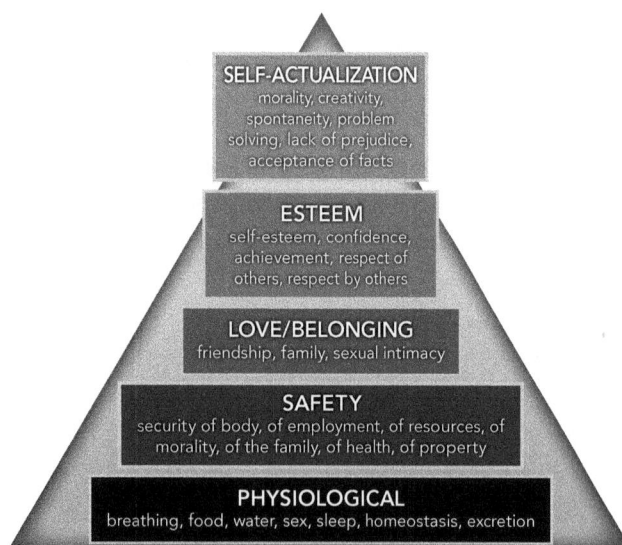

### Hierarchy of Needs

The Leadership Maturity approach is based on research and observation that, over time, people tend to grow and progress through a number of very distinct stages of awareness and ability. One of the most well-known and tested developmental models is Abraham Maslow's *hierarchy of needs*—a pyramid visual aid Maslow created to help explain his theory of levels of human needs, both psychological and physical. As you ascend the steps of the pyramid you can eventually reach a level of self-actualization.

*Figure 1.3 Maslow's Hierarchy of Needs*

Leadership Maturity develops much like other capabilities in your life. Building on your Leader Type, you continue to grow, increasing access to or capacity for additional skills. We call this "transcend and include," in that you transcend the prior maturity level yet still maintain the ability to function at that maturity level. Let's use the example of learning how to run to illustrate the process of development. You must first learn to stand and walk before you can run. And yet, as you eventually master running, you still effortlessly retain the earlier, foundational skill that allowed you to stand and walk. It is also important to note that while individuals develop the ability to run, there are many times that walking is a more appropriate choice of movement. The successful leader has a broad repertoire of behavior and is able to select the most appropriate one depending on the situation.

New maturity levels can develop gradually over time or emerge quite abruptly, and people develop through maturity levels at vastly differing rates that are influenced by significant events or "disorienting dilemmas." Those events or dilemmas provide opportunities to experience your world from a completely different point of view. The nature of those influential events can vary greatly, ranging from positive social occasions like going to college, moving to a new place, marriage, a new job, or the birth of a child, to negative experiences, such as job loss, an accident, or death of a loved one. These situations often trigger lasting changes in how you think and fee

Adding to the complexity of developmental growth is the fact that the unfolding of Leadership Maturity is not based on age. Some developmentally advanced people may be relatively young, while others may experience very little developmental growth over the course of their lives.

We apply leadership maturity when we listen and exchange ideas with others, employ introspection, and display openness to learning. Most people naturally intuit what motivates or challenges others. We believe a solid understanding of Leadership Maturity is critical to innovating leadership. While the purpose of this workbook is to introduce you to the concepts of developing leadership, we encourage you to delve into these ideas in much greater detail.

## Resilience

There are two distinct ways to understand Resilience. First, using an engineering analogy, resilience is the amount of disturbance a system can absorb before a breakdown occurs. From a leadership perspective, Resilience is adapting to erratic change with fluidity and endurance; as a result, resilient leaders see challenges as opportunities rather than threats. As a leader, addressing all aspects of Resilience is critical to your well-being and your ability to function at high levels.

Resilience is unique in that it integrates the physical and psychological aspects of Leader Type and Leadership Maturity to create the foundation of a leader's inner stability. This foundation, this inner stability enables you to adapt to ongoing changes common during your college years and early in your career. As a college student, you may feel that your life is in a constant state of flux, requiring you to acclimate to new situations time and time again. Perhaps you experienced one of these changes in the past year—moving away from home, choosing a major or career path, starting or ending a relationship, or taking on a new leadership role or position within a student organization, internship, or job. Each of these experiences can affect your well-being, and being resilient is essential to successfully navigating those changes.

Resilience is closely connected to well-being. You have likely considered the concept of well-being as it relates to being physically fit. Colleges and universities typically educate students with messages about healthy eating, exercise, and other issues of wellness. You might not have considered the impact of being well on your role as a leader. The underlying premise is this: As a leader, you need to be physically and emotionally healthy to do a good job. As a leader, you are a role model to those following you. Studies have indicated that high levels of team productivity are positively related to high levels of well-being among members of the team. By role modeling self-care, flexibility, and adaptability, you will lead more effectively and your followers will become more resilient as well.

The resilient leader also has a sense of purpose and strong supportive relationships. When working hard to achieve goals and complete tasks (both main points of focus for college students, and whether those tasks are for academic pursuits, job, family responsibilities, or leadership roles on campus), it is easy to forget the importance of nurturing relationships with those who are important in our lives. Many college students forge new friendships while still navigating old ones that are changing and evolving. Students often find themselves in new group roles and living in a community atmosphere for the first time (residence halls and student organizations are great examples of these new groups). All of this change means that developing positive relationships are crucial during this complex life stage. Developing resilience is a combination of focusing on personal well-being and creating positive support through interpersonal relationships.

It is likely you have heard the term "emotional intelligence." The concept of emotional intelligence (EI) has been used to coach leaders by having them focus on a healthy awareness of their own emotions and the emotional needs of others. EI is now recognized as being as significant as traditional IQ measurements. Those whose emotional intelligence levels are high are successful in both their personal and professional lives. There is an excellent emotional intelligence assessment written specifically for college students that you can purchase to help you explore your own growth areas around emotional intelligence.

*Emotionally Intelligent Leadership: A Guide for Students* walks readers through the three facets and nineteen capacities of emotional intelligence as they relate to leadership development, and helps students process through their assessment results. By spending time reflecting on capacities like emotional self-control, flexibility, developing empathy, managing conflict, and assessing the environment, you can build upon existing capacities, develop awareness of areas of personal growth, become more keenly aware of the emotional needs of others, and build your own resilience for overcoming challenges. We recommend that you consider taking this assessment along with the others recommended during the course of this workbook. As you will note below, emotional intelligence is a key component of our resilience model. You can use your results later in your self-reflection activities.

## Fig. 1.4 Elements of Resilience

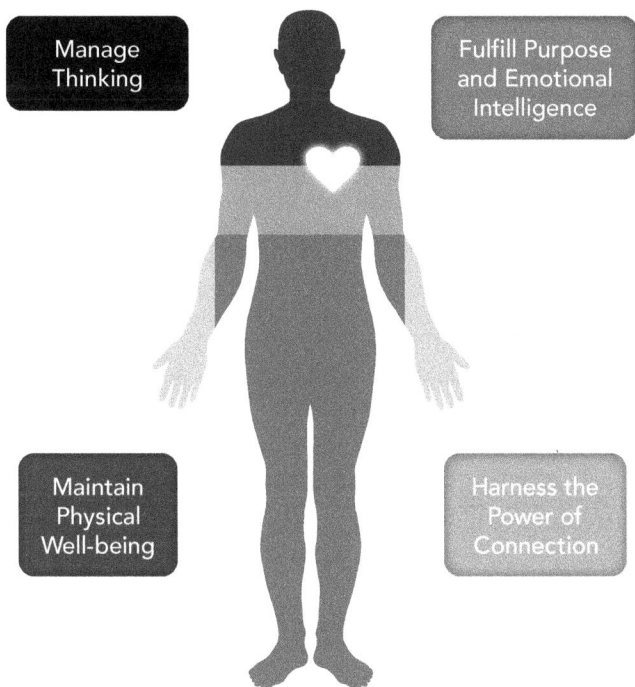

Manage Thinking

Fulfill Purpose and Emotional Intelligence

Maintain Physical Well-being

Harness the Power of Connection

Based on what you've read, it is clear that the underlying premise of Resilience is that leaders need to be physically and emotionally healthy to do a good job. In addition, the resilient leader also has a clear sense of life purpose, strong emotional intelligence, an effective capacity to manage thinking, and strong supportive relationships. For most people, enhancing resilience requires a personal change.

Our model has four categories, shown in Fig. 1.4. They are: Maintain Physical Well-Being, Manage Thinking, Fulfill Purpose Using Emotional Intelligence, and Harness the Power of Connection. These categories are interlinked, and all of them must be in balance to create long-term Resilience.

Leaders (especially college student leaders) often say they are too busy to take care of themselves. When balancing classes, work, and student leadership responsibilities, there is often little time left in the week. For some students, having a good week means simply that you got your checklist completed and you feel good about what you accomplished—but there must be a balance between self-care and meeting daily commitments. Over the longer term, you will make choices for your Resilience and personal health, or against it. Our message is that creating and maintaining resilience is essential to your success. As you improve your ability to be resilient, you will think more clearly and have a greater positive impact in your interactions with others; investing in your Resilience supports not only your personal effectiveness, but will lead to greater success as a leader.

The following table provides questions for each of the four Resilience categories to identify opportunities for improvement.

## TABLE 1.1 KEYS TO BUILDING & RETAINING PERSONAL RESILIENCE

**Maintain Physical Well-being**

Are you getting enough:

- Sleep
- Exercise
- Healthy food
- Time in nature
- Time to meditate and relax

Are you limiting or eliminating:

- Caffeine
- Nicotine

**Fulfill Life Purpose**

Understand what you stand for. Maintain focus. Ask:

- What is my purpose?
- Why is it important to me?
- What values do I hold that will enable me to accomplish my purpose?
- What opportunities do I have within the context of a college or university that can help me achieve my life purpose?

**Manage Thinking**

Practice telling yourself:

- Challenges are normal and healthy for any individual or organization
- My current problem is a doorway to an innovative solution
- I feel inspired about the opportunity to create new possibilities that did not exist before

**Harness the Power of Connection**

Practice effective communication:

- Say things simply, and clearly
- Make communication safe by being responsive
- Encourage people to ask questions and clarify if they do not understand your message
- Balance advocacy for your point with inquiring about the other persons' points
- When you have a different point of view, seek to understand how and why the other person believes what they do in a non-threatening way
- When in doubt, share information and emotions
- Build trust by acting for the greater good

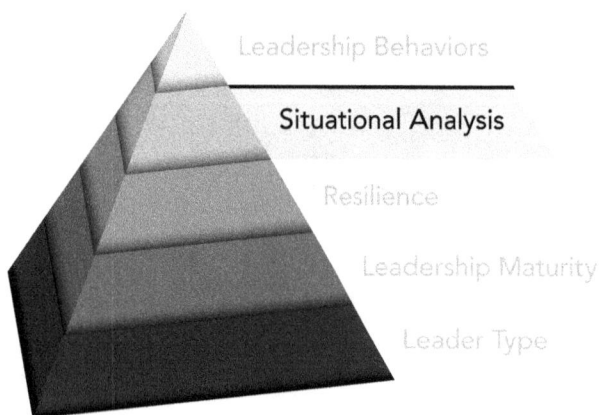

## Situational Analysis

Though much of the work of building innovative leadership is based on an in-depth examination of your personal experience through activities, school, and employment, understanding the background or context of that experience is equally important. Consider that your experience is not merely a collection of personal expressions, events, and random happenstance; rather, it is fundamentally shaped by the background interplay of your individual attributes, shared relationships, and involvement in organizations.

Every moment of experience is influenced by the interaction of self, culture, action, and systems. All four of these basic dimensions are fundamental to every experience we have. Situational Analysis involves evaluating the four-dimensional view of reality shown in figure 1.5. This comprehensive approach ensures that all dimensions are aligned, resulting in balanced and efficient action. We refer to these four dimensions as self, action, culture, and systems. This balance—without favoring individual elements—is an important skill for innovative leaders.

Leaders often take a partial approach to changing organizations. They over-emphasize systemic change with little or no consideration of organizational culture or of how their personal views and actions shape the change. This multi-dimensional approach provides a more complete and accurate view of events and situations. Situational Analysis enables you to create alignment across the four dimensions on an ongoing basis.

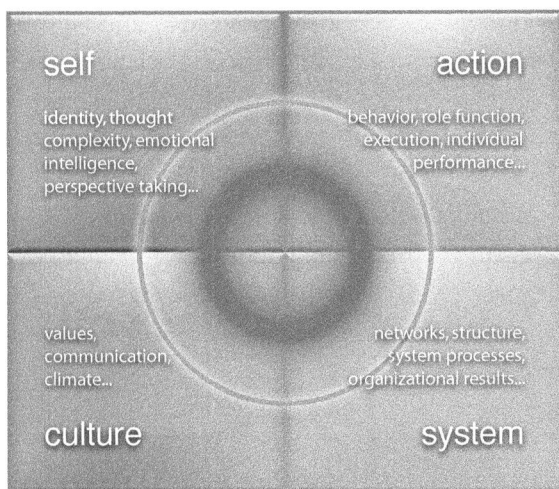

**Figure 1.5 Integral Model**

## Integral Model

American-born philosopher Ken Wilber developed a conceptual scheme to illustrate the four basic dimensions of being that form the backbone of experience. His Integral Model provides a map that shows the mutual relationship and interconnection among four dimensions where each represents basic elements of human experience.

When you use Situational Analysis, you are cultivating simultaneous awareness of all four dimensions. Let's look at an example. This is a sample narrative taken from *Integral Life Practice* (Wilber et al) and refined to reflect student experiences that will give you a more comprehensive description of how these dimensions shape every situation in your life.

**Example:** *"Visualize yourself, in a newly elected role, walking into your first student organization meeting. You are responsible for running the meeting that day…"*

**Self** *(Upper-Left Quadrant, "I")*: You feel excited and a little nervous. Thoughts race through your head about how best to prepare.

**Culture** *(Lower-Left Quadrant, "We")*: You enter a familiar organizational culture of shared meaning, values, and expectations that are communicated, explicitly and implicitly, every day.

**Action** *(Upper-Right, "It")*: Your physical behaviors are obvious: walking, waving hello, opening a door, sitting down conversing casually with organization members, and so on. Brain activity, heart rate, and perspiration all increase as the start of the meeting draws nearer.

**System** *(Lower-Right, "Its")*: Years of work by previous student leaders in your role have led to this moment, the faculty advisor, who has been an advisor for the organization for 10 years walks in the door, the student union just e-mailed you about the funding policies for this fiscal year.

Developing your capacity to be aware of all dimensions of reality in any given moment and identify misalignments is a crucial part of continually innovating leadership. Even though you cannot physically see the values, beliefs, and emotions that strongly influence the way an individual friend or colleague perceives himself and the world, nor a group's culture, emotional climate or collective perception, they still profoundly shape the vision and potential of leaders to innovate.

Situational Analysis is an innovative leadership tool that not only allows you to make more informed decisions, but also helps you optimize performance within yourself, your teams, and the broader organization. The alignment of all dimensions is the key to optimizing performance.

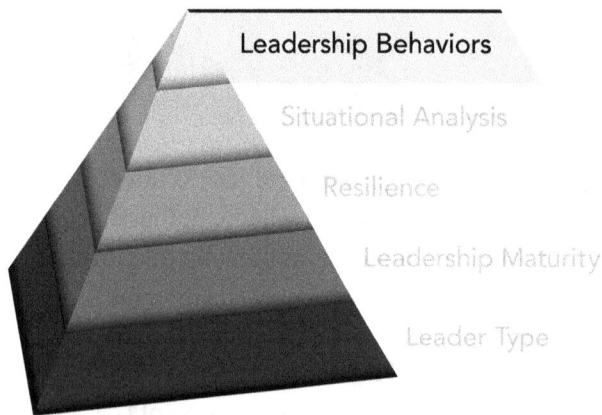

## Leadership Behaviors

Industry-specific skills, knowledge, and aptitudes are essential to success in a particular field of work or within a specific organization. In addition, learning to adapt leader behavior to a specific organizational culture is an essential element of innovative leadership. This section is about actionable and observable leadership capability, organization or field specific knowledge, appropriate skills and their associated behaviors.

Leadership Behaviors are important because they are the objective actions the leader takes that impact organizational success. Again and again, we have seen brilliant leaders behave in a manner that damages their organization, and we have seen other leaders consistently behave in ways that promote ongoing organizational success. Effective Leadership Behaviors drive organizational success, while *ineffective* Leadership Behaviors drive organizational dysfunction or failure. Even the most functionally brilliant leader must demonstrate effective Leadership Behaviors to be successful.

A successful leader must possess knowledge of organizational administration and the essential Leadership Behaviors. As a student you have opportunities to learn how organizations function. If you are involved in a student organization, volunteer to serve as the organization's liaison to the university staff, or volunteer to serve on university-wide committees as a student representative. Most college campuses have opportunities within academic departments or student life departments for students to get involved. Learn how the funding models work and how decisions are made that affect students. Acquiring some awareness of how decisions are made, who the stakeholders are, and how the hierarchy is structured will give you great transferable knowledge for your future career. Early in a leader's career, a mastery of organizational leadership sets him apart from his peers.

Leadership Behaviors are also important when learning to effectively work in teams and groups. As a leader, your natural tendencies and behaviors impact everyone around you. It is easy to forget that your natural way of thinking and working is unique. This can lead to conflicts or misunderstandings that could impact your perception as an effective leader. It is imperative that you are keenly aware of your behaviors in teams and groups and how those behaviors intersect with the behaviors of others.

It is important that you gain greater self-awareness of your typical response to situations, how you behave in moments of stress and conflict, and your unique approach to problem solving. Later in this workbook you will have an opportunity to take a number of assessments, and one specifically that helps you identify your natural behaviors in team and group settings. This self-understanding is vital to your future as a leader because how you are perceived by others can often impact your ability to lead. If you are perceived as a self-aware leader who understands multiple perspectives and approaches and as someone who is open to other ways to behave or approach tasks, then you will likely be highly regarded as a leader.

The following model reflects leadership traits of highly-advanced leaders. These are leaders who demonstrate significant maturity, including the ability to engage employees and make a significant impact on an organization. While we understand that this book is written for students, we have included the full list with the expectation that this will provide a set of behaviors to work toward now and in the future. The competencies in this list will help you to begin identifying people you think are strong leaders. You can observe them, ask them to become mentors, and integrate some of their behaviors into your current or future development plans.

| STRATEGIST COMPETENCY MODEL | | |
|---|---|---|
| **Competency** | **Explanation** | **+/−/↑** |
| Professionally Humble | ***Cares about getting it right more than being right***<br><br>■ Holds personal and organizational mission as a guide and focal point for where to invest energy in service of leaving a legacy<br><br>■ Cares more about the organization and the result than a personal image<br><br>■ Freely, happily, and instinctively gives credit to others<br><br>■ Puts principles ahead of personal gain | |
| Unwavering Commitment to Right Action | ***Is unstoppable and unflappable when on a mission***<br><br>■ Has the ability to be fully committed, hard driving, fully focused, and yet not perceived as being myopic or stubborn<br><br>■ Has the ability to 'stay the course' when under pressure | |

| Competency | Explanation | +/–/↑ |
|---|---|---|
| 360 Degree Thinker | **Has the "Balcony View"**<br><br>- Innately understands the systems, constraints, perceptions, near-term, long-term, and secondary impacts of strategy and decisions—and how to transform them to complete amazing results<br><br>- Balances competing commitments of multiple constituents on a regular basis<br><br>- Thinks in terms of systems, dialogues, and transformations when focusing on constraints and perceptions—considers the organizational context when making recommendations<br><br>- Commits to continual personal learning and building learning systems<br><br>- Understands cross organizational impact, striving to understand the interconnection across multiple complex systems and make highly informed decisions considering implications across broader contexts<br><br>- Integrates personal insights into organizational systems as one of the many decision criteria | |
| Intellectually Versatile | **Has developed interests, expertise, and curiosity beyond the job and organization**<br><br>- Interested and involved with areas beyond their comfort zones<br><br>- Aware of and interested in political, national, and international developments<br><br>- Uses external interests to enhance legacy and provide balance in life | |
| Highly Authentic and Reflective | **Highly focused on personal behavior**<br><br>- Dedicated to personal growth and development and growing and developing others<br><br>- Maintains a strong personal growth regimen and honors insights emerging from that practice<br><br>- Surprisingly non-defensive and open to feedback<br><br>- Seeks discussions and feedback even in uncomfortable situations<br><br>- Manages emotions in the most difficult situations—understands the impact and contagious nature of emotions so is able to develop skills to recognize them, manage/metabolize them and relate to others productively<br><br>- Preserves perspective in times of stress, taking a long term view and remaining vision focused, they are less challenged by difficult situations than others<br><br>- Demonstrates emotional courage—willing to confront challenging situations<br><br>- Investigates ways to enable the organization to improve its ability to meet its mission more efficiently and effectively | |

| Competency | Explanation | +/−/↑ |
|---|---|---|
| Able to Inspire followership | **Has the special ability to connect with people at all levels of the organization to create a shared vision**<br><br>■ Understands change intuitively, the steps to manage change, and how to help the organization overcome resistance to change<br><br>■ Diffuses conflict without avoiding or sidestepping the source of the conflict<br><br>■ Uses humor effectively to put people at ease<br><br>■ Relates to a broad range of people and understand their motivators and stressors<br><br>■ Connects projects to the individual goals while working to overcome barriers<br><br>■ Provides valuable feedback to others in a manner that supports their growth and development<br><br>■ Acts consistently in a manner that is perceived as fair | |
| Innately collaborative | **Welcomes collaboration in a quest for novel solutions that serve the highest outcome for all involved**<br><br>■ Seeks input from multiple perspectives—valuing diverse points of view<br><br>■ Creates solutions to complex problems by creating new approaches that did not exist, pulling together constituents in novel ways, creating broader and more creative alliances<br><br>■ Understands that in a time of extreme change, input from multiple stake holders with diverse points of view are required<br><br>■ Integrates insight and wisdom into overall balancing of multiple perspectives | |

In looking at this list, you may feel a bit overwhelmed. This is a lot to ask of a single person! We recommend that you look through the list and consider which behaviors already come naturally to you. Put a plus (+) next to those behaviors. Then, read through the list again and put an upwards-facing arrow (↑) next to any of the statements where you think improving on that behavior would improve your skills as a leader. Consider this self-assessment in later chapters as you determine where you would like to develop yourself in the next year. In addition, later in the workbook when you take the *StrengthsFinder* assessment, you will be asked to return to this list and consider how your natural talents and strengths can help you build on the behaviors you desire to improve. Tapping into your natural abilities to build on those that are more challenging for you is a great way to structure personal development.

You may also notice that many of these behaviors are described as occurring within the context of a group. If you don't already have a group setting where you have an opportunity to lead and practice these behaviors, find one. Again, join student organizations on campus, volunteer to take the lead on planning an event for your residence hall, or simply step-up to help lead a group project in class.

If you are not sure where to find these opportunities, seek assistance from a staff member at the university. Most staff members in student services areas will be excited to help you find opportunities to match your interests and leadership goals. You can simply contact the student activities or campus engagement office and ask to make an appointment to talk with a staff member. Your academic advisor may be able to help guide you in the right direction as well. Take advantage of the many opportunities a college campus affords and utilize the staff who are there to help you grow and learn.

## Developing Innovative Leadership

Chapters two through seven walk you through the process of developing innovative leadership as a college student leader. Each chapter reflects one step in the development process and includes tools, templates, questions for reflection, and an example from a student who completed the process. The comprehensiveness of this reflection coupled with the exercises will give you insight into yourself and your organization. Leadership development is an ongoing process. Figure 1.7 below shows the six steps in the process of innovative leadership development.

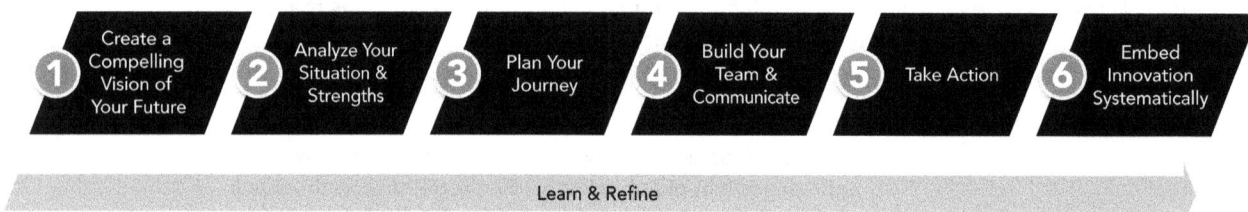

**Fig. 1.7 Leadership Development Process**

While this process appears linear, we have found that leaders often return to earlier parts of the process to clarify or improve various components. The structure of our process will challenge you to refine the work you have accomplished in prior tasks. First ideas are often good ones, but when you work with this tool you will continually find insight and discover new things.

The time you spend on the workbook is an investment in your development. If you are engaging deeply in the process it will likely take you three to six months or longer to complete. Whether considering your first steps as a new college student or as an experienced leader on campus, reflection and thorough evaluation are required. This reflection will take time and is critical to your growth. We strongly encourage you to engage in the process with as much time and attention as possible. The value you ultimately take from this process is closely linked to the time you invest.

# REFLECTION QUESTIONS

What innovative challenge does your organization face?

▰▰▰▰▰

How does your organization support effective leadership
for innovation and change?

▰▰▰▰▰

In what ways would you consider yourself an innovative leader?

▰▰▰▰▰

How do you personally connect with leadership and innovation?

▰▰▰▰▰

Where are the opportunities for you to be an innovative leader?

▰▰▰▰▰

What would make you and your organization more effective in
leading innovation during a time of significant change?

▰▰▰▰▰

If you were successful beyond your wildest dreams in
becoming an effective leader, what would happen? Write the
story as though it is a newspaper article with your name in the
title of the article, "Dr. (Your Name) Has Been Celebrated
as a Highly-Effective Leader."

# CHAPTER 2

The Innovative Leadership Workbook is designed to provide a step-by-step process to support you in developing your own innovative leadership capacity. The field book that serves as the foundation for this workbook has been tested with a broad range of graduate and undergraduate students.

These tools differ from many others by directing you through an exploration that takes into account your unique, individual experience while simultaneously considering the groups and organizations to which you belong.

## Step 1: Create a Compelling Vision of Your Future

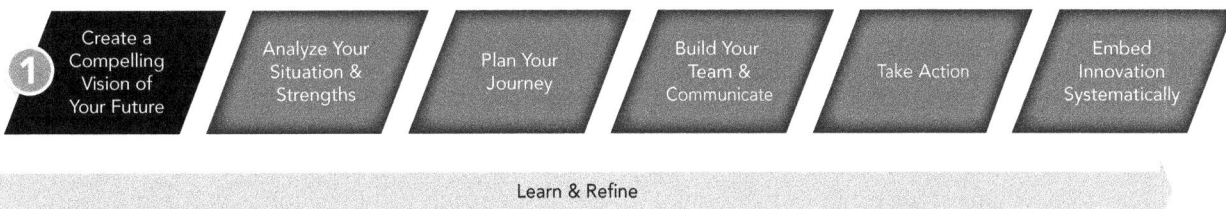

| 1 Create a Compelling Vision of Your Future | Analyze Your Situation & Strengths | Plan Your Journey | Build Your Team & Communicate | Take Action | Embed Innovation Systematically |
|---|---|---|---|---|---|

Learn & Refine

Your roles will change over the next few years at a rapid pace so the first step in starting your development process is cultivating a sense of clarity about your overall vision, which can also be summarized as your direction and aspirations. By knowing your vision and aspirations, you are equipped with information that helps you align the energy you invest with the work you do. The intention behind your aspirations fuels both personal and professional goals, as well as provides a sense of meaning in your life. When your actions are aligned with your goals, they drive the impact you create in the world at large. As you move forward in the visioning process, we will guide you to begin thinking about individuals or groups who inspire or significantly influence you.

Simply put, your vision and aspirations help you decide where best to invest your time and energy, and clarifying them helps you define a manner of contributing to the world that authentically honors who you are. Your vision and aspirations further help you clarify what you want to accomplish over time. You can select the time span that resonates for you, whether short-term—one to five years—or perhaps a longer-term time horizon, such as the span of your lifetime.

Some students become overwhelmed when considering long-term vision. It becomes exhausting to hear and answer the question, "So what do you plan to do after graduation?"—especially if you are completely unsure of your future. Try not to let this visioning activity cause you anxiety. It is okay if you are unsure of your future career path. Choose a shorter length of time for your focus and view this exercise as a way of setting goals to better yourself personally (learn new skills, develop greater confidence in your abilities, learn your style of leadership, consider applying or an internship, etc.). Set a vision that you are comfortable with, but that also challenges and stretches you. After clarifying your own unique, personal vision, you will have the foundation for the change process. Knowing your vision and values creates the basis for your goals, and can help you align your behavior with your future aspirations.

As part of the visioning process, it is important to consider the context of your contribution and your leadership role, your organization, or your community. If you are clear about your personal vision, you can evaluate where and how to go forward.

In addition to creating a well-defined vision, it is also important to be clear about your motivation. The combination of vision and desire will enable you to maximize your potential. Without sufficient desire, solid vision, and understanding of your current capabilities, you are likely to struggle when progress becomes difficult.

## Tools and Exercises

The exercises and reflections will guide you in identifying what is most important to you. You may want to consider what you want to do professionally, as well as the type and extent of the impact you want to have on the world. If you are unsure of a future career path at this time, simply choose one of the paths you are considering. Remember, you can always circle back to this reflection your direction changes. One note to consider: many students experience dissonance when determining a future vision because what they truly want is not what society or their family supports. We encourage you to use this section of the workbook to think through any tensions or expectations that may impact making decisions about your future. It is important that you consider what you want. If you are following a path determined by others, this will not be an authentic reflection process for you. For example, exploring a dream of using your artistic abilities in your future career as part of this exercise doesn't mean that you will decide on this interest, but it does give you a chance to consider that this path might look like.

It is important to note that many will complete this exercise and still not have a clearly articulated vision—this is because defining personal vision requires a great deal of introspection for most of us. While some people grow up knowing what they want to do for a living, others find that identifying a vision is a process of gradual exploration and will take more time and energy than completing a single workbook exercise. You will likely refine your vision as you progress through later chapters in the workbook based on the information you learn about yourself. You will likely continue to modify your personal vision over the course of your professional career and even your life. Because the visioning process is iterative in nature—a process of self-discovery—the exercises in this book will serve as the foundation for a longer process that may take considerably more time to complete. It is highly unlikely that you will even stay on the career path that you originally choose in college. Research has indicated that people tend to change careers seven times throughout the course of their lifetime. Know that this exercise is not setting you on a thirty to forty-year path. Your vision might go as far as ten years out and that is enough.

## Define Personal Vision

Follow the steps defined below:

**Step 1: Create a picture of your future.** Imagine yourself at the end of your life. You are looking back and imagining what you have done and the results you have created.

- What is the thing of which you are most proud?

- If you had a family, what would they say about your strengths and greatest talents?

- What would your friends say about you?

- What did you accomplish professionally? (Consider this with the lens of a specific career, or without a specific career in mind, as well as particular attributes or goals that you wish to achieve. For example, you can say that in your career you want to be known as a great mentor—this is not career specific, but is perhaps an important aspect you seek in a future career)

> *"I am proudest of how my work inspired millions of people to chase dreams and goals they previously thought to be impossible."*
>
> —Eric Philippou

For the rest of this exercise, let that future person speak to you and help you set a path that will enable you to look back with pride and say things like, "I feel fulfilled and at peace. I lived my life well."

**Step 2: Write a story.** Now that you have that image of what you will accomplish, write a brief story about your successful life. Include details about the questions above. Make it a story of what you went through to accomplish each of the results for the questions you answered. What you are trying to create is a roadmap that gives you more insight into what you would want if you had the option to design your perfect life.

- Who helped you along the way?

- What did you enjoy about your daily life?

- Who was closest to you?

- Who were your mentors?

- What feelings did you have as you accomplished each milestone along the way?

- How did you mentor others and contribute to the success of others?

- What did you do to maintain your health?

- What role did spirituality or religion play in your journey?

- What job(s) did you have?

- What role did material success play in your life?

- What type of person were you (kind, caring, driven, and gracious)?

**Step 3: Describe your personal vision.** Given the story you have written and the qualities you demonstrated, write a two to five sentence life-purpose statement—a statement that talks about your highest priorities in life and your aspirations. This statement should capture the essence of how you want to live your life and project yourself.

> ***An example*** - *My vision is to develop myself to my greatest capacity and help others develop and thrive in all aspects of their lives. I will live consciously and courageously, relate to others with love and compassion, and leave this world better for my contribution.*

**Step 4: Expand and clarify your vision.** If you are like most people, the choices you wrote are a mix of selfless and self-centered elements. People sometimes ask, "Is it all right to want to be covered in jewels, or to own a luxury car?" Part of the purpose of this exercise is to suspend your judgment about what is "worth" desiring, and to ask instead which aspect of these visions is closest to your deepest desire. To find out, ask yourself the following questions about each element before going on to the next one: If I could have it now, would I take it?

Some elements of your vision don't make it past this question. Others pass the test conditionally: "Yes, I want it, but only if…" Others pass, but are later clarified and distilled in the process. As you complete this exercise, refine your vision to reflect any changes you want to make.

After defining and clarifying your vision, it is time to consider your personal values. The combination of these two exercises will help you create the foundation of what you want to accomplish and the core principles that guide your actions as you work toward your vision.

## Checklist for Personal Values

Values are deeply held views of what we believe to be worthwhile. They come from many sources: parents, religion, schools, peers, people we admire, and culture. Many go back to childhood; others are taken on as adults. Values help us define how we live our lives and accomplish our purpose.

**Step 1: Define what you value most.** From the list of values (both professional and personal), select the ten that are most important to you—as guides for how to behave, or as components of a valued way of life. Feel free to add any values of your own to this list.

## TABLE 2.1: PERSONAL VALUES CHECKLIST

- Achievement
- Advancement and promotion
- Adventure
- Arts
- Autonomy
- Challenge
- Change and variety
- Community
- Compassion
- Competence
- Competition
- Cooperation
- Creativity
- Decisiveness
- Democracy
- Economic security
- Environmental stewardship
- Effectiveness
- Efficiency
- Ethical living
- Excellence
- Expertise
- Fame
- Fast living
- Fast-paced work
- Financial gain
- Freedom
- Friendship
- Having a family
- Health
- Helping other people
- Honesty
- Independence
- Influencing others
- Inner harmony
- Integrity

- Intellectual status
- Leadership
- Location
- Love
- Loyalty
- Meaningful work
- Money
- Nature
- Openness and honesty
- Order (tranquility/stability)
- Peace
- Personal development/learning
- Pleasure
- Power and authority
- Privacy
- Public service
- Recognition
- Relationships
- Religion
- Reputation
- Security
- Self-respect
- Serenity
- Sophistication
- Spirituality
- Stability
- Status
- Time away from work
- Trust
- Truth
- Volunteering
- Wealth
- Wisdom
- Work quality
- Work under pressure
- Other: _____

**Step 2: Elimination.** Now that you have identified ten values, imagine that you are only permitted to have five. Which five would you give up? Cross them off. Now cross off another two to bring your list down to three.

**Step 3: Integration.** Take a look at the top three values on your list.

- How would your life be different if those values were prominent and practiced?

- What does each value mean, exactly? What do you expect from yourself, even in difficult times?

- Does the personal vision you've outlined reflect those values? If not, should your personal vision be expanded? Again, if not, are you prepared and willing to reconsider those values?

- Are you willing to create a life in which these values are paramount, and help an organization put those values into action?

Which one item on the list do you care about most?

## *Putting Vision into Action*

After defining and clarifying your vision and values, the next step is to reflect on how to put them into action. You will consider the things you care about most, as well as your innate talents and skills, to determine what about your current life you would like to refine or change. You are probably passionate about specific interests or areas within your life; if you're really fortunate, you will have opportunities to participate in one or more of those areas.

The purpose of this exercise is to consider how best to incorporate your passions into how you make a living. You likely have passions that will always remain in the realm of hobbies; the main point of the exercise is to move closer to identifying your passions and expressing them in as many areas of life as possible.

> *"Love is my #1 value, because excellence (#2) and meaningful work (#3) both stem from love. Love for my daily life consists of meaningful and skillful work."*
>
> —Eric Philippou

In our experience, part of figuring out what you want to do is paying attention to what you find profoundly interesting. Those interests simply reveal themselves in the course of your daily interaction with peers and colleagues, and quite frequently in the way you choose to spend your time outside of class. They are reflected in whatever you find yourself reading; they even display themselves in the context of more casual occasions, and are often seen in activities shared among friends.

This is the type of exercise that appears very simple on the surface, and may be something you revisit annually in order to refresh what is genuinely important to you. We find that revisiting allows you to nurture a sense of continual clarity about your direction. Iteration provides a mechanism for clarifying your direction as you grow and develop. With everything you try (false starts and all) you will discover a deeper truth about yourself that moves you closer to your most authentic passions. Some of those passions will be incorporated into your career; other passions help shape your personal life.

## Exercise: Putting Vision into Action

**Step 1: Identify your foundation.** *Answer the three questions below by compiling a list of responses to each.*

- What are you passionate about? This will come from the prior exercise and should now be relatively concise.

- What meets your economic needs?

- What can you be great at?

*\*Note: your answers to these questions should reflect your values from the Personal Values Checklist.*

**Step 2: Review and identify overlap.** *Review your answers and identify the overlaps.*

### Vision-Based Actions

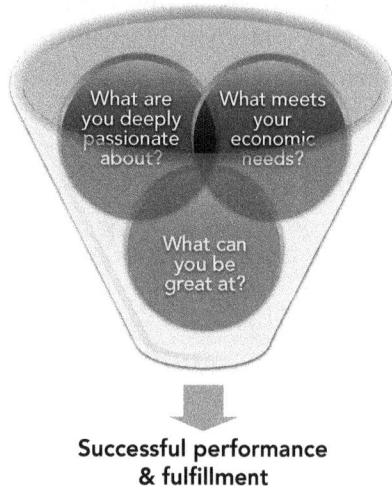

What are you deeply passionate about?

What meets your economic needs?

What can you be great at?

**Successful performance & fulfillment**

**Step 3: Harvest the ideas.** Based on the overlaps, do you see anything that might be incorporated into what you do or how you work? This could mean adding additional extra-curricular activities, a new job, or a new project to your current life. Having an opportunity to act on your values is key to your development as a leader.

An example of this is a student who, based on significant reflection, learned he valued giving back to the community in a way that he was not doing. He was studying and working which left limited time to give back. This exercise and the reflection questions helped him see that if he wanted to live his values, he would find small ways to be of service even while attending school and create a plan he could live with during each phase of his life. In the process of following his passion, he is building the habits that will position him to not only succeed in work but also build his reputation as a civic leader over the course of his career.

## Real World Application

### Be Part of Something Great

As you begin to develop a vision of your future and become an innovative leader in this world, understand that there are countless things you can do and groups you can join right now that will bring you closer to your long-term goal. If you haven't already joined a group or student organization, or haven't checked out possibility for a job/internship related to your future goals, put this book down, search for a group, contact current group members about joining, and then come back to this page.

Being part of a group that aligns with your goals is essential to becoming a leader in your desired field. Understand that a true innovative leader is one who influences positive change in a group, even if he or she is not the formal appointed "leader," so don't be deterred by the fact that you're a new member. The information in this book will prove to be priceless if you are actively part of a group that aligns with your future goals.

## Personal Experiment

Write down your answers to the above exercises as you complete them, and consider them to be a rough draft. Then, summarize it with three bullet points:

- your personal vision,

- your main personal values

- your plan of action

Live by these bullet points for the next few days, and pay close attention to any changes in your life, such as your productivity, mood, etc. Then, see how you can refine or improve your bullet points, even if you already satisfied with how things are. This is not only a great way to refine the overall vision of your future, but also to establish a habit of trial and error—because becoming an innovative leader requires developing and testing hypotheses like a scientist, that is, measuring, learning, and refining on an ongoing basis.

## Innovative Leadership Reflection Questions

To help you develop your action plan, you need to further clarify your direction using the reflection questions below. "What do I think/believe?" reflects your intentions. "What do I do?" questions reflect your actions. "What do we believe?" reflects the culture of your organization (i.e., work, school, student organization, community), and "How do we do this?" questions reflect systems and processes for your organization (organization refers to student organizations, company where you work as an intern, sports teams, and social groups). You may be involved in multiple organizations, so we recommend you select only one and use it consistently for all reflection questions. This exercise is an opportunity to practice innovative leadership by considering your vision for yourself and how it will play out in the context of your life. You will define your intentions, actions, culture, and systems in a systematic manner.

Table 2.2 contains an exhaustive list of questions to appeal to a broad range of readers. You will likely find that a few of these questions best fit your own personal situation. Focus on the questions that seem the most relevant to you. We recommend you answer one to three questions from each category.

---

### TABLE 2.2: QUESTIONS TO GUIDE THE LEADER AND ORGANIZATION

**What do I think/believe?**

- How do I see myself in the future? What trends do I see around me that impact this view? Have I considered how these trends impact the way I contribute?
- How does my view of myself impact me? Am I inspired by my vision? Terrified?
- How do I see myself within the larger environment? This can range from my family, a student organization, to the global environment.
- After doing the exercises, what is my vision?
- After doing the exercises, what are my values? What do I stand for? What do I stand against?
- What are the connections between my career vision and my personal mission, passion, and economic goals?

**What do I do?**

- How do I gather input from key supporters to incorporate into my vision (family, friends, classmates, coworkers? How do I assess what I learn from others or know about myself?
- How do I research trends that will impact my major/industry so I can understand my future placement and how to navigate potential transitions in my industry?
- How do I synthesize competing goals and commitments to create a vision that works for me in the context of the communities I serve (family, friends, work, and community)?
- How do I develop my vision taking the greater economic conditions into account?
- What do I tell others about my vision? Do I have an "elevator speech"? Is it something I think is inspirational?

**What do we believe?**

- How does my personal vision fit within the larger context of my family, my college organizations or activities, my community, my internships, or my desired job?
- How do I create a shared belief that my vision will help the organization succeed within the larger community, and also help the community succeed?
- What do we believe we stand for as an organization? How should we behave to accomplish what we stand for (guiding principles/values)? Do my values align with the organizational values?
- How do I reconcile differences between my values and those of my organization? How will these differences impact my ability to develop toward my vision and goals?

**How do we do this?**

- How do I monitor the organization's impact on my vision? How do I honor my vision when helping define/refine the organizational vision?
- What is our process for defining/refining changes to our shared vision for the organization and other systems I function within? What is our process for clarifying and documenting our values? How do I ensure that my values are aligned with our guiding principles?
- Who gives me feedback on their perspective of my progress? How often? What form would I like this feedback to take?
- What measures help me determine progress toward my vision and values? How do I track and report progress toward these goals? Is my behavior supporting the organizational goals? Are the organizational goals supporting my goals?

---

Because there are many different ways to relate with the workbook, we offer three case studies. Our student leaders have either answered different questions, or approached the exercises in slightly different ways to demonstrate the range of options for working with the exercises. We recommend you find the approach that best meets your needs and fits your style.

To help illustrate these reflection questions, we've included Anthony's, Shelby's, and Kelly's answers. We have tried to capture their internal thought processes in these exercises so that you can see the direction they each take toward personal development.

## Case Study: Anthony

*Anthony is an undergraduate student at Capital University. As of this writing, he is a college senior majoring in business and is a member of the school's baseball team. Below, are Anthony's candid answers to the reflection questions.*

**Step 1: Create a picture of your future.** *Imagine yourself at the <u>end of your life</u>. You are looking back and imagining what you have done and the results you have created.*

- *What is the thing of which you are most proud?*

  Looking back the end of my life, I am proud of what I accomplished over my lifetime. I have lived my life with a purpose to be, first, a good person, then a great father, and finally have contributed to society through my career in business. I have had a job that made me wake up happy every day, and that I never considered to be a "chore." I have provided for my family and have been able to help others in my chosen profession to achieve their best. I am most proud of how I was able to balance my time between being a successful businessman and time with family and community. Others would say that I worked hard for everything I got, but that I also was not afraid to take every opportunity presented to me that allowed me to be a life-long learner. I am able to look back and say that I tried to be prepared for whatever life threw at me, and that I took situations and turned them into opportunities.

- *If you had a family, what would they say about you?*

  If I had a family, they would say that I was hard working and persistent, and that I would have done anything to provide for them. I would have taught them core values in life and would have done my best to help each of my children to be successful in whatever they would have wanted to do in life. I believe they would say that I was "there," and that I participated in their lives each and every day. I would hope that they had seen me as someone who did not shy away from a challenge, and as a father who cared deeply about them.

- *What did you accomplish professionally?*

  I completed two summer internships in business and marketing. As a triple major, I was academically focused. I was also a four-year letter college baseball player. These accomplishments demonstrated my drive to succeed. At the end of my life I can say that I was able to integrate what I learned about business in school with life experience. I was in a position of leadership and was humbled to have served those who worked for me. I had a staff that looked to me for guidance and leadership in their careers while maintaining high ethical behaviors. I strove for, and accomplished, attaining the role of senior vice president or president of my own or another company. I worked in a field that had a hands-on approach to business, manufacturing or a sports equipment company. I accomplished my dream of being senior vice president of Rawlings or Louisville Slugger. I continued my education, getting my MBA or CPA certification. I gave back to my profession by mentoring and helping to develop others starting out in the field.

■ *What would your friends say about you?*

Many of my friends would say that I was hard working, could never sit still because I always had to be doing something, consistently strove for excellence, fun, was caring, and got work done right and on time.

For the rest of this exercise, let that future person speak to you and help you set a path that will enable you to look back with pride and say things like, "I feel fulfilled and at peace. I lived my life well."

**Step 2: Write a story.** *Now that you have that image of what you will accomplish, write a brief story about your successful life. Include details about the questions above. Make it a story of what you went through to accomplish each of the results for the questions you answered. What you are trying to create is a roadmap for your journey that gives you more insight into what you would want if you had the option to design your perfect life.*

■ *Who helped you along the way?*

I was fortunate to have had many people help me through life. Some of the individuals who influenced me were my family, friends, coaches, and professors. The most significant people who helped me along life's path were my parents, my wife and my children. My parents were the ones that guided me and gave me the basic skills in life to understand the difference between right and wrong. They taught me a strong work ethic and always to strive to be my best and to evaluate others based on their actions, not preconceived biases based on conjecture. They taught me that prejudice is damaging. My wife was the one who went through everything with me and supported me in every decision I made early in my career after college. My wife helped me understand that the world was bigger than me and that I was part of a team. We learned how to grow together and made decisions based on mutual goals and dreams. My children played a key role in some of the decisions I made about the future, and helped me to be thoughtful in my decisions and to think before I spoke. My children helped me understand that I had to have stamina and endurance in order to be a role model and to always make time for them. (Looking back, now I realize there were many days when my own father had to be tired after a long day at work, but we never realized it because he always spent time with us as a family.) My children and family helped me realize that it was the quantity of the time I spent with them and not necessarily the quality that made a difference. I don't think life can always be planned and scheduled, so quantity of time seemed more important to me. I learned that "life happens" and it was all the little things I did with my wife and children that really mattered. I believe these lessons of thoughtful decisions, patience, and truly caring about people were what helped me in the business world.

■ *What did you enjoy about your daily life?*

I enjoyed being around my family that I loved and cared about. I enjoyed waking up every day and looking outside and thinking "I can't wait to get out there." I enjoyed spending time with family and friends who were close to me and making them laugh and smile. I enjoyed sitting at the dinner table and hearing what everyone did that day, and laughing about some of the funny things that happened. Every day there was something new to learn or a new task to tackle. As a kid, those challenges taught me different life lessons, like having to work together with my brother and sister as a team to accomplish what was expected around the house. I enjoyed simple experiences, that are not necessarily planned and scheduled, and having close friends to talk and do things with each day. I enjoyed having a profession that, even though tough at times, was always stimulating and never seemed like work.

■ *Who was closest to you?*

Looking back on my life, my wife and children were the people who were closest to me and with whom I spent the most time. My wife and I always made decisions together about our family in the moment and for the future. We relied on each other to get through the good, the bad, and the ugly aspects of life. The others closest to me were my parents, friends, aunts, uncles, and grandparents.

■ *What feelings did you have as you accomplished each milestone along the way?*

Each milestone in my life brought different challenges. I felt that I was on the right path to be successful from the start after college. I had a great support structure around me in my family, girlfriend, and friends. I felt a sense of pride each time that I took the next step in my life, whether it was graduating high school or moving on to college. Each step made me nervous, but with happy anticipation and being thankful for those who helped me along the way. I had not realized that the steps in life come and go so quickly before suddenly I was setting out into the world on my own. When I graduated college, I was not even sure what type of business I wanted to work in or in what city. This was the scariest time in my life. My girlfriend had another year of school in Columbus, Ohio, yet my home city was Cleveland. My career decisions were based on which position had the most potential for growth. Feeling proud and sure was what I felt when I was offered the first position in which I would be making a living and setting out on my own. But, when faced with the first day on the job, my certainty was replaced with insecurity about what I really knew about business in the workplace and if I could I turn the theory of textbook into reality. Each step in my life, from getting my first job, to getting married and having children had components of anxiousness, fear, and excitement.

■ *How did you mentor others and contribute to the success of others?*

As a college student, I had many different opportunities to become a leader and mentor. One opportunity was during group projects where we had to work in teams. I felt I could use my five Gallup strengths to better the group and find each person's strength so that the group could reach its full potential. Being able to help lead a team during group projects led to a smooth running project and, in turn, led to a good grade for the class. Another mentoring opportunity was on the baseball field. Talking to the new guys coming in as freshman—not only about baseball, but, also the classes that they were taking, college life in general, and which professors I got the most from—was a chance to advise and connect, and made me feel that I was helping them to be successful both on and off the field.

■ *What did you do to maintain your health?*

Being a college athlete meant continuously working out, and I kept that habit throughout my life. I enjoyed exercise, being active, and working outside. I never smoked or chewed tobacco when I was younger and did not start after college. I ate as healthy as I could, but also rewarded myself by occasionally indulging in foods that weren't so healthy. My family always sat down to dinner, and we ate "three square meals" a day, well-balanced and healthy, another custom that I kept throughout my lifetime. Managing stress was accomplished through exercise and having several hobbies that I enjoyed, including woodworking and fishing.

■ *What role did spirituality or religion play in your journey?*

My faith was an important foundation. By living my faith as fully as I could by attending church service and listening to scripture, I was able to pray about tough times and know that I would be led to the right path. Attending church every weekend was a constant throughout my life. Giving the God that I believe in one hour of one day a week was nothing compared to what I have been given. I am proud to have raised my family with the same faith base that I grew up with. There were times when I questioned my faith, but then relied on it to help me through the most difficult times. As I grew older I understood the meaning behind my faith and tried to live my life each day using those teachings as my guide.

■ *What job did you have?*

I had a career path that took me in several different directions. My first job out of school was in sales and marketing. The job market was tight, so I found the best possible position I could at the time. The path I took always involved continuing education in my field. I would try to learn all aspects of the business I was working in, not just the sales and marketing area. I followed my mentors into several job changes that gave me increasing responsibilities and expectations. I had to make a decision fairly early between getting my MBA or my CPA, and chose the MBA since I felt it would give me the broadest approach to business while incorporating some aspects of accounting. I rose through my company's ranks and became a supervisor within seven years. I worked in a manufacturing division of a sporting goods company. I enjoyed interacting with other departments especially research and product development. Through my interest in new product design and manufacturing, I was offered an opportunity to lead a new division that would help design and test products in the professional sports arena. I am currently retired from that company, but enjoy being a consultant for the division that I helped create.

■ *What role did material success play in your life?*

Material items have had importance at points in my life. I was fortunate to start working at a young age and making what I thought was very good money. I liked to have nice things and paid more for something of quality rather than purchase something cheaply made. Material items did not play a big part in my life, but were often necessities. After I graduated from college I started to experience what truly living on my own meant. Needing the basics of a place to live, transportation, and food to eat became very apparent. At the time, I thought meeting my needs on a monthly basis was material success. However, I realized that each step of my life required increased material needs. Eventually getting married and buying a house was a big step in the realization that I needed a plan to grow my wealth to support my family. When I look back on my life, I can say that we never were what would be thought of as poor, but we did not spend money we did not have. Family time and vacations were important to us, so we budgeted our money to be able to do that each year. I never had to have the biggest house on the block or the fanciest car, but did buy high quality items when I needed them. Ironically, now at the end of my life, when I can afford those high-priced things I don't think of them as very important.

■ *What type of person were you (kind, caring, driven, and gracious)?*

I would say I was a combination of kind, caring, driven, and gracious, but, if I had to rank them in order, I would have to say that driven was number one. I had a tendency to be very focused and driven regarding things that I liked or was working on. In my job I was the type of person who helped others advance in their career. I was a good mentor and advocate for those who worked for me and was always honest with those that needed to improve. I think being kind to others by treating them as I wanted to be treated was important. I maintained these traits over the course of my life and professional career.

**Step 3: Describe your personal vision.**

My vision right now in life is to graduate college and get a job that I will enjoy so that I can help the people around me and have a positive impact on them. In addition, I will strive to be the best person that I can be and work to have a positive impact on others' lives.

**Step 4: Expand and clarify your vision.**

My vision is to use the knowledge I have acquired as a graduate from college and impact those around me in a positive way by demonstrating that you can do anything you put your mind too. I will be a motivator and mentor to help others reach their full potential.

## Anthony's Checklist for Personal Values

**Define what you value most.** There are so many different elements in life that I value. The top ten values most important to me are; family, religion, happiness in daily life and my work, good friends, my health, learning for experiences, hard work, success, trustworthiness, and empathy.

**Elimination.** Now that you have identified ten values, imagine that you are only permitted to have five. Which five would you give up? Cross them off. Now cross off another two to bring your list down to three. The remaining three are:

Family, happiness, and good health

**Integration.** *Take a look at the top three values on your list. Based on your responses, answer the following question:*

- ■ *How would your life be different if those values were prominent and practiced?*

The top three values on my list are: family, happiness, and good health. I think that happiness is based on my ability to integrate the other values that are important in my life. My life would be different and less meaningful if I didn't focus on the top three values because they are the foundation of my life. Having good health is crucial for being able to maintain an active and enjoyable life with my future wife and children. My happiness will affect my family's happiness and I need to be able to step back and think about any mistakes I have made and be a strategic thinker about how that affected my future. Happiness is based on not making the same mistakes twice in my life. I would look at each day as a new opportunity to make these three values prominent in my life as a way to live a happy life.

- ■ *What does each value mean, exactly? What do you expect from yourself, even in bad times?*

Family means the most to me for so many different reasons. One is that I know that they are reliable and consistent in their actions and beliefs. My family has done so much for me and I can always count on them to help me, guide me, and teach me. Even when I don't achieve success, my family is always there for me when I need them the most. Happiness is an approach to life, an outlook. I prefer to look at the glass as half full, rather than half empty. Learning from my experiences is one of the most valuable assets that I can have in my life. It helps me to avoid making the same mistake twice and allows me to progress in my field of studies by learning from my own experiences and also from the experiences of others. Even when a situation is not going as planned, I can always learn something from it which allows me to maintain a generally positive (happy) outlook. Good health. I have been an athlete my entire life. I believe that people who take care of their physical bodies are able to think clearer and perform better. As I go forward in life, I expect to maintain my focus on health by being physically active and focusing on healthy food.

- ■ *Does the personal vision you've outlined reflect those values? If not, should your personal vision be expanded? Again, if not, are you prepared and willing to reconsider those values?*

I believe that my personal vision defines who I am and what I continue to strive to be in the future. Those are the three values that I have learned from, counted on, and can rely on for the rest of my life. Not only are these three important, there are many more that extend from the basic core values in my personal vision statement.

- ■ *Are you willing to create a life in which these values are paramount, and help an organization put those values into action?*

I am one-hundred percent confident in my own personal vision and am willing to create a life in which these values are paramount both personally and professionally.

- ■ *Which one item on the list do you care most about?*

I care deeply about the family component of my value system and personal vision. I believe that my family has provided the basic support system for how I live my life and I am confident that has set me on the right path to achieve my other values. The family relationships established in my upbringing are the basis for all my actions and the decisions I make.

## *Putting Vision into Action Exercise*

**Step 1: Identify your foundation.** Answer the three questions below by compiling a list of responses to each.

■ *What are you passionate about?*

While I have many passions in life, the most prominent are friendships with family and friends, playing baseball, being outdoors, and working on projects such as building things with my hands and acquiring new knowledge, my faith, and being able to help others. I am passionate about, and dream of, starting my own company someday. The business courses I have taken in college are exciting since they are teaching me the direction and specifics needed to achieve my dreams.

■ *What meets your economic needs?*

I would like to find a position in business that has the potential for growth with increasing responsibilities and pay. A position in marketing and sales in which I can use my abilities to teach my customers about the products and services I represent would be a good first step right out of school. My economic needs will be met by landing a good first job that will allow me to make enough money to start paying off my student loans, be able to live comfortably on my own, and have extra money to explore new activities and do things that I enjoy.

■ *What can you be great at?*

For years my family and friends have been telling me that I would be a good teacher. While my major is business and marketing, I believe I could be great at using the basic skills of teaching to form relationships with others in business. Business and marketing is about creating value for your products or services in the minds of your customers. A large part of creating this value is based in teaching the customer why they should invest in your product or service. Having a good educational plan about your product and being able to deliver the message in a way that is understood is crucial for success in business. So, in a sense, I need to be a great teacher to be successful in business.

*Note: your answers to these questions should reflect your values from the Personal Values Checklist.*

**Step 2: Review and identify overlap.** From the three questions "what I can be great at," "what meets my economic needs," and "what am I passionate about" there are not many that overlap, but they do correspond with my personal vision and values. One of the largest overlaps is teaching and relationship building. I can use my strong financial and marketing background to form relationships that allow me to help my customers accomplish their financial goals. This allows me to help others, make a good living, and do something I can be great at.

**Step 3: Harvest the ideas.** At this stage in my life I am going to be graduating soon with majors in marketing, leadership and management, and accounting. I am beginning to apply for jobs and thinking about the next five to ten years with regard to where I will be and what professional position

I will hold. The concepts surrounding professional growth through the development of both personal and professional relationships has to be part of my equation, especially in the business world.

## Anthony's Answers

### What do I think/believe?

- **How do I see myself in the future? What trends do I see around me that impact this view? Have I considered how these trends impact the way I want to contribute?**

I have seen trends in business such as a growth in the accounting field since the implementation of Sarbanes Oxley and the growth of social media marketing. These trends will impact my career choices in that what is available in the future will be different than even what was available when I entered college. Social media has changed how business is conducted and I anticipate those changes to grow over time in some ways that we cannot imagine right now. I see myself as a life-long learner who incorporates what I have learned in each phase of my career and experience, and applies what I have learned to make decisions about the future. I will be willing to take calculated risks to meet my professional expectations based on business trends. My desire to be a lifelong learner is a real asset because the trends will require me to continually learn and stay current. In addition to the need to continue learning, professional relationships with professors, mentors at internships, and fellow students in the business program help formulate my immediate circle of influence in business. Additionally, support and guidance from family and friends will be important to my future upon graduation.

### What do I do?

- **How do I gather input from key stakeholders to incorporate into my vision (family, business, self)?**

It is important for me to gather information and input from family members regarding traditions and religious obligations. My faith and religious beliefs are established through my family and reinforced through actions and behaviors. I will work hard to obtain the trust of others through behaviors that reinforce my reputation as someone who is dependable and keeps their word. It will become easier to make decisions, both personally and professionally, as I accumulate experiences. I will always be willing to ask questions and evaluate the answers to see if they fit my personal vision.

I also gathered input from my college advisors, coaches, and key professors about where to focus my studies so I could select a career that would be aligned with my skills. I have had several professors who know me and my skills well. I will also rely on my family as they know me better than others.

## What do we believe?

■ *How does my personal vision fit within the larger context of my family, my college organizations or activities, my community, my internships, or my desired job?*

My vision is to use the knowledge I have acquired as a college graduate and to influence those around me in a positive way by demonstrating that anyone can do anything they put their mind to. I will be a motivator and mentor to help others reach their full potential.

My personal vision is aligned with the greater context of my life with my family, friends, coaches because they all value success and working hard. They helped me create the belief that I need to work hard, and also that it is my responsibility to mentor and help others reach their full potential.

Where I am in my life right now going through college and applying for jobs will influence me for the rest of my life. Getting the grades that I need to succeed and learning from mistakes that I have made in the past will play a big role in my success. Being trusting and trustworthy in multiple ways with my family, coaches, professors, interviewers, and friends are all part of my personal goals and vision.

■ *How do I create a shared belief that my vision will help the organization succeed within the larger community and also help the community succeed?*

I believe that accomplishing the basics of my vision plan will aid an organization in being successful. It is difficult at this stage in my life to share an in-depth vision with others outside my family because my primary focus right now is to complete college and apply for jobs. I do believe my commitment to learning and building relationships will aid an organization and the larger community for the better. Presently, my organization and community consists of my family, friends, and the community of students that I share classes with. I realize through this exercise that in a short period of time (upon graduation) my community will expand as will my influence on the immediate community and beyond.

■ *What do we believe we stand for as an organization? How should we behave to accomplish what we stand for (guiding principles/values)? Do my values align with the organizational values?*

Until I graduate and move on to the workplace, I consider my college as my organization. Like me, the university values furthering education, developing experiences that will help drive future decisions in a logical manner, and encourages hard work, a sense of community, and building relationships. However, the university values families and friends in a different way than I do. Even though they accept students for who they are, there is not the bond that is formed through years of shared experiences. The university is in the business of education, and must operate as such, thus needing to demonstrate values that parents and students find important to attract them to the school.

■ *How do I reconcile differences between my values and those of my organization? How will these differences impact my ability to develop toward my vision and goals?*

My personal values and the values of the university have several differences. My relationships and community are based on interacting with people who share my values and goals. The university has a broad sense of community and accepts all students regardless of their values. Both the university and I seek to form relationships that last into the future, however, not all of the values of the college align with my goals and values. My end goal is to graduate from the university and have a successful career in business. The university's goal is to prepare students for the future and prepare them for the real world.

## How do we do this?

■ *Who gives me feedback on their perspective of my progress? How often? What form would I like this feedback to take?*

Many people throughout my lifetime have given me feedback on my progress. Some examples are: family members, coaches, professors, friends, and peers. I would say that my family gives me the most feedback with regard to all aspects of my life: education, social, and family dynamics. I believe there is a fine balance of when to give or expect to get feedback on progress. Certainly I expect it from my family after I have completed a task and asked for feedback so that I can evaluate what I have done. Professors give feedback on a regular basis through testing and projects. Coaches give more immediate feedback during practices or games and may make decisions before any explanation is given on any changes. The form of feedback that I prefer to receive is face to face and immediate. In that way I can work to make any necessary changes to improve or advance my progress in a more efficient manner based on the feedback. I will incorporate all aspects of feedback, both positive and negative, to assure that I do not make the same mistake twice and learn from each experience (my second personal value).

■■■■■■

## Case Study: Shelby

*Shelby is a senior at The Ohio State University studying English and Communication. She is from a small town in Ohio and wants to work in the field of Education after graduation.*

**Step 1: Create a picture of your future.** *Imagine yourself at the <u>end of your life</u>. You are looking back and imagining what you have done and the results you have created.*

■ *What is the thing of which you are most proud?*

Looking back on my life, I lived a fun, love-filled life. I didn't care how much money I made; I cared about how much time I spent with the people I loved. I am proud of the impact I made in people's lives through kindness and support. My pride is from memories I have with my husband and our children, going on adventures, laughing, and spending time together. The things of which I am most proud are less measurable and are things felt, cherished that withstand the sands of time.

■ *If you had a family, what would they say about you?*

My husband: My wife was the most selfless, kindest person I knew. I loved the way she embraced everything wholeheartedly and unapologetically. Her zest for life is what drew me in when we first met and what will keep her spirit alive forever in our hearts.

My children: Mom was SO MUCH FUN. Between her singing, dancing, and constant silliness, we never had a dull moment in our house. Mom loved life. She loved birds in the backyard, to the owner at our favorite brunch place, to us. We appreciated how her love made us feel.

My brother: Shelby lived the life she built for herself. She worked hard to achieve exactly what she wanted out of life. She refused to back down from a challenge and never let negativity from anything get her down. My sister never ceased to inspire me to do more and be more. She supported me in everything since day one, and I will hold that close to my heart forever. She was a caretaker, a fighter, and a phenomenal woman.

■ *What did you accomplish professionally?*

I attained a high level position at a university working to create an exceptional experience for future college students.

At 24, I graduated with my master's in education and completed my time with Teach for America in Indianapolis. I thought that I would be a teacher forever, but was presented with the opportunity to work in education through schools and nonprofit organizations in Columbus, Ohio. Eventually, I was offered a great position at a large university, where I was also asked to begin the pursuit of my PhD in Higher Education Administration. I became Dr. Shelby at 35 and worked in various leadership and teaching roles, loving every second of university faculty-staff life.

■ *What would your friends say about you?*

My friends would say I was FUN and tell you that I was one of the most alive people they knew. My friends will say I loved people and animals and beings and it showed through the strong, loving relationships I maintained throughout my life.

For the rest of this exercise, let that future person speak to you and help you set a path that will enable you to look back with pride and say things like, "I feel fulfilled and at peace. I lived my life well."

**Step 2: Write a story.** *Now that you have that image of what you will accomplish, write a brief story about your successful life. Include details about the questions above. Make it a story of what you went through to accomplish each of the results for the questions you answered. What you are trying to create is a roadmap for your journey that gives you more insight into what you would want if you had the option to design your perfect life.*

■ *Who helped you along the way?*

I was held, guided, pushed, and led by people. Really, really good people. I would like to highlight a few of these amazing human beings to emphasize how they changed my life.

My mother raised my brother and me by herself. She is the most dedicated, hardworking person I know. She did not simply teach us good table manners and how to tie our shoes, she also taught us how to work for what we want out of life and to be relentless and tenacious. She taught me the value of this life and continues to hold my hand and laugh with me.

My brother is five years my junior. We grew up playing with hand-me-down Barbie dolls and garage sale Ninja Turtles, and old swing sets in the backyard. Sean was my first friend as a child and remains one of the most consistent, close friends I have. Without knowing, he pushes me every day to do more, be more, and strive for more out of life. My mom built the engine for my relentlessness and Sean is the accelerator that drives it.

Early in my adult life, two of my high school teachers saw potential in me that I hadn't seen in myself. In my senior year, I was given the responsibility of being the first and only chemistry TA because they knew I loved chemistry and wanted to major in it. When I changed my major to English and realized I wanted to teach after college, they welcomed me back to their classrooms as an observer and treated me like a colleague.

In college, I was blessed with a fairy godmother/#1 supporter/when-you-need-life-given-to-you-straight-you-go-to-her-person in my life. She knew me from Day 1 of my college journey. I was so intimidated by everyone and everything, and wasn't sure if I was going to make it. I have asked her for so much, and I have appreciated every ounce of her leadership in my life. Not only has she led me through college, but also she has been my friend.

- ### *What did you enjoy about your daily life?*

Coffee – Bright sunny mornings out dusty
windows, rolled down – Long hair blowing, cut
for My Kids.

People – Big smiles rosy cheeks from
laughing, too much – Time spent apart, but
we Still Love.

Ohio – The only place where truly
people love you – Where coffee brews, and
you Feel Home.

- ### *Who was closest to you?*

My family: Husband, children, mom, brother, grandparents; my college family including close friends and members of student organizations.

These people were my foundation and my ego control panel. They were the ones to build me up and to take me down when I need it. I consider the people closest to me to be the ones who have guided me. We laughed together, cried together, and were there for everything in each other's lives.

■ *What feelings did you have as you accomplished each milestone along the way?*

My first reaction (to most things in life, honestly) was to be excited. It was not until after I thought about it and overanalyzed everything that the fear set in. After I psyched myself out, determination crept up and told me I could and would do anything I strove for. This came from the really, really good people in my life who contributed to my learning to believe in myself.

■ *How did you mentor others and contribute to the success of others?*

In high school I thought I was a great mentor because I was really good at talking to people and building people up, but I learned in college that sometimes a great mentor is the one who sits back and listens quietly. The power of listening comes with practice and purpose; I did not learn its difficult nature until my senior year in college in capstone leadership class. To me, the first "step" in mentorship is building a relationship, a friendship. You have to have mutual like and trust in order to ask for advice or offer it. After the bond is strong, then conversations and questions flow naturally over coffee, ice cream, or a walk down your favorite street.

■ *What did you do to maintain your health?*

Throughout high school I was very active in sports like volleyball, softball, and cheerleading and I knew when I went to college I was going to need to step up my workout game to maintain the physical health. I started going to the student recreation center and took advantage of the variety of fitness classes available. I found that exercise helped me not only physically, but also it helped me reduce and deal with stress and anxiety.

My mom always said "everything in moderation," which is how I look at nutrition. I never wanted to deprive myself of anything—a cupcake, a glass of wine, or pizza. But, over time, I grew to realize the importance of eating MORE veggies, lean meats, and fruit. Eating more of these foods just made me feel better all around.

■ *What role did spirituality or religion play in your journey?*

I have a tattoo of a very simple black-line cross on the outside of my left ankle. To me, this symbolized my faith in the best way for me. The cross symbol is obvious, Jesus died on the cross for us, and I believed that wholeheartedly. I got it on the left side of my body because that is where our hearts are located. Why the foot/ankle region? I believe my faith guided every step I took in my life in some way. My beliefs were liberal and maybe not always the most popular with the majority, but the way I saw it, a very deeply personal relationship with my God made sense for me.

■ *What job did you have?*

I spent some time working with nonprofit organizations that focused on access to education, especially for first generation college students. Later, I began working at a university and worked my way around many positions within the university. I retired as the Senior Vice President of Advancement at a large university.

■ *What role did material success play in your life?*

As a child, I always dreamed of a big house, fancy cars, and lots of money. I did not have much growing up, so these big fancy things seemed like something I could only dream up and pretend I had. As a grown woman I did not need much to be happy. I wanted a cute apartment and a car that worked. Throughout job changes and income changes and kids and life, I remained that same woman. I did not want anything big and fancy; I wanted lots of fun people around and the space and time to foster that. My home was for housing family and friends and my car got me to the place of work I loved so much. Material "goods" was not something I ever really saw as "success."

■ *What type of person were you (kind, caring, driven, gracious)?*

I was kind-hearted and showed love to people all my life. My students, my coworkers, my husband, my own children, my family and friends, and even strangers in restaurants received my kindness and a warm smile.

I was the type of person who felt what other people were feeling in a deep, meaningful kind of way. When my children cried, I felt their pain. When my husband was upset, I felt his anger and emotions. I considered empathy to be one of my gifts.

Never one to allow anyone to tell me "no" when I wanted to achieve something, I was hardworking and driven. I ran head first into every challenge I was faced with and took every step to achieve exactly what I wanted. I never let another's negativity or discouragement infect my goals or let me lose sight of what I wanted in life.

As a positive person, I saw a world filled with beauty. I never let the ugliness of people's words and actions change how I saw things or did things in my life.

**Step 3: Describe your personal vision.** *Given the story you have written and the qualities you demonstrated as a person, write a two to five sentence life-purpose statement—a statement that talks about your highest priorities in life and your aspirations. This statement should capture the essence of how you want to live your life and project yourself.*

My life is one that reflects positivity. My aspiration is that when one encounters me, they feel joy and happiness.

**Step 4: Expand and clarify your vision.** *If you are like most people, the choices you wrote are a mixture of selfless and self-centered elements. People sometimes ask, "Is it alright to want to be covered in jewels, or to own a luxury car?" Part of the purpose of this exercise is to suspend your judgment about what is "worth" desiring, and to ask instead which aspect of these visions is closest to your deepest desire. To find out, ask yourself the following questions about each element before going on to the next one: If I could have it now, would I take it?*

*Some elements of your vision don't make it past this question. Others pass the test conditionally: "Yes, I want it, but only if…" Others pass, but are later clarified and distilled in the process. As you complete this exercise, refine your vision to reflect any changes you want to make.*

*After defining and clarifying your vision, it is time to consider your personal values. The combination of these two exercises will help you create the foundation of what you want to accomplish and the core principles that guide your actions as you work toward your vision.*

When I was writing my personal vision, I didn't think of anything material. Now that I'm thinking more deeply, I definitely want some material, self-centered things out of life like a new car and a nice house. I know that if I am able to do what I love every day and get to come home to people I love, my vision will be fulfilled.

## Shelby's Checklist for Personal Values

**Step 1: Define what you value most.** (in the order of which they came to mind)

Personal relationships, health/fitness, spirituality/faith, family, friends, loving and being loved, responsibility, music/art, curiosity and interest in the world, gratitude

**Step 2: Elimination.** *Now that you have identified ten values, imagine that you are only permitted to have five. Which five would you give up? Cross them off. Now cross off another two to bring your list down to three. The remaining three are:*

Personal Relationships, Health/Fitness, Spirituality/Faith

**Step 3: Integration.** *Take a look at the top three values on your list.*

▰ *How would your life be different if those values were prominent and practiced?*

It would be amazing to be able to solely focus on personal relationships, my health and fitness, and my faith every day of my life. If I could concentrate 33 percent of my life and attention to all the people I care about and love, 33 percent to my personal health, and 33 percent to my spirituality, life would feel balanced and equal in a way. However, I am also the type of person who embraces the chaos and feel like if I didn't have the other seven things I value, I would be missing out on some of the excitement of this life.

▰ *What does each value mean, exactly? What do you expect from yourself, even in bad times?*

1. Personal relationships are the bonds I have with other amazing humans in my life. I count family, friends, mentors, teachers, professors, and friendly people I meet all in the realm of personal relationships. Obviously, some of these relationships are significantly stronger and longer-lasting than others, but I am a person who thrives off of other people and their energies.

2. Health and fitness were values I grew up with and were instilled in me from a young age. My mom, brother, and I always had balanced, healthy meals. We went for walks and played tennis and our mom encouraged us to always be involved in a sport. I value my health so much as I'm getting a little bit older and watching the older members of my family slowly deteriorate because they did not take care of themselves when they were young. I recently had a health scare with my thyroid and this was a huge wakeup call for me to really get on track with working out and eating well. In complete honesty, sometimes health and fitness go out the window in bad times. Wine, ice cream, and romantic comedies are a great cure for sadness sometimes. But I have found that also in bad times, a good, long run is a cure that works just as well.

3. Faith has always been huge for me. In good times and in bad, I find myself in prayer and talking to God. It's that simple for me in my mind and my heart. Good times, *Thanks, God!* Bad times, *I need you, God!* My spirituality and faith follow me everywhere I go like a good accessory, covering my heart and guiding my feet.

▰ *Does the personal vision you've outlined reflect those values? If not, should your personal vision be expanded? Again, if not, are you prepared and willing to reconsider those values?*

I definitely think the vision I have set out is aligned with my values in a really beautiful way. In order to live a life that reflects positivity, I must live every day with a positive mindset. I need good people and good relationships in my life. In order to be passionate, I have to have a guiding force with which I discover my passions (read: faith). In order to drown in joy at work, I have to have a career I am passionate about and have worked hard to achieve. In order to live life with humor and style, I have to take care of myself and be able to enjoy my life.

▰ *Are you willing to create a life in which these values are paramount, and help an organization put those values into action?*

Yes! I am confident in my vision and willing to create a life where these values are paramount and help any organization.

▰ *Which one item on the list do you care most about?*

Personal relationships are at the top each time for a reason, obviously. When I think of what I value most in life, I think of people—people I love, people I know, people who have helped me, people I've served.

## Putting Vision into Action Exercise

**Step 1: Identify your foundation.** *Answer the three questions below by compiling a list of responses to each.*

■ *What are you passionate about?*

I am passionate about people. I am passionate about my opportunity to attend university. College was my saving grace in life. The university and the people at the university saved me from the tiny world I existed in before I became part of the community.

I am passionate about helping others in simple ways like picking up dropped items in line and giving them back, holding doors, saying kind things to strangers. My passion lies in making people feel loved and important.

■ *What meets your economic needs?*

I want my passions and my job to collide into a beautiful constellation that will pay the bills. If I have a job I like and am good at and can pay the bills I owe, my economic needs will be met. As I grow and change jobs, I hope to make enough money to not only meet basic economic needs, but also to give back to my alma mater. I have always dreamed of creating a scholarship for a student from my hometown community so that another's hope to attend college can become a reality.

■ *What can you be great at?*

I can be great at anything I put my mind to, right? I think people are naturally gifted in many different areas, but we don't all always get the chance to use these gifts. Dreaming big, I can be great at giving TED Talks. I'm gifted in public speaking and getting people to listen when I speak. More realistically, I can be a great mother, gifted with traits of love and kindness.

*Note: your answers to these questions should reflect your values from the Personal Values Checklist.*

**Step 2: Review and identify overlap.** *Review your answers and identify the overlaps.*

I see overlap in words I used. I see the word passion, people, and love repeated. I think these words paint a picture of what I am becoming: someone who is an advocate, a lover, and gives back to her community, her people.

**Step 3: Harvest the ideas.**

I see passion and love in my English and communication majors because I am very passionate about reading and books, as well as public speaking. As an educator, I will foster my passion for people and my ability to love deeply. I pray I can take my passions and my experiences back to my alma mater one day in a leadership role to give back to the university that brought me this far.

### Shelby's Answers

### What do I think/believe?

- *How do I see myself in the future? What trends do I see around me that impact this view? Have I considered how these trends impact the way I want to contribute?*

Trends I see in our life focus on wellness and happiness in the workplace—especially the university system. As we look at expectations of the millennials, they are much more focused on social responsibility, ecological healing and purpose. I believe in love and in living out your passion. I believe in hope and helping those without it. I think the trends we read about will materialize and organizations have the environment in which I want to work.

Let me create the picture I have in my head of my future self:

The sun is waking me and my husband up, as is the pitter patter of little feet coming down the hallway. Our kids are always up before we are so they can come and dive bomb into our bed. We have coffee and breakfast together and the kids to go school. We spend time with our families often and, when possible, we spend time in nature.

My husband and I go to work. I head to my university job where I work with an amazing staff of professionals equally as passionate as I am. We have fun at work, and get things done to better the university.

### What do I do?

- *How do I gather input from key stakeholders to incorporate into my vision (family, business, self)? How do I assess what I learn from others or know about myself?*

I am a person who asks for advice and asks for help, but I don't always do this. I used to be apprehensive and afraid to ask for help, but time has turned me into a person who needs others to make my vision come true. I rely on "my gut" for a lot of decisions, as I see this as a form of divine intervention in my life. Phone calls with my mom, texts with friends, and talking to God are how I gather input to make my vision my reality.

### What do we believe?

- *How does my personal vision fit within the larger context of my family, my college organizations or activities, my community, my internships, or my desired job?*

Obviously, my love of prose influences most of what I write, and certainly how I feel. Poetically, my personal vision is this:

Within my community, it is not enough simply to be, I must also be aware. I must experience and feel what my community feels.

Within the context of my family, I give and receive compassion. It is what drives us to be fully human. And, how can we be human without seeing the humor in life? Humor helps to keep all in perspective.

My work is my passion, and my passion is my work. I have a unique style in expressing my passion in my work.

■ *How do I create a shared belief that my vision will help the organization succeed within the larger community and also help the community succeed?*

I think the first step to creating a shared vision is waking up every day of my life and making sure I am clear on what my vision is and how I want to live it. When I have mastered my vision in my own mind and my own life, I will then be able to share it with others. I don't necessarily believe that I need to go into my first staff meeting and declare *Here is my vision….blah blah blah.* I want to live in a way where people can FEEL what is important to me through a simple conversation and interaction. I want to radiate love and my capacity to love into my workplace, so people will feel confident in living out their own visions and the vision of our community as a whole.

■ *What do we believe we stand for as an organization? How should we behave to accomplish what we stand for (guiding principles/values)? Do my values align with the organizational values?*

As a senior, I am fairly certain that my next step will be to take a teaching position with Teach for America. As a member of TFA, I will do my best to wholeheartedly live out the mission and the values set forth for all children.

Teach for America's Mission is simple—providing excellent education to all children. In order to make this mission happen for all children, TFA believes that there are 5 Core Values to live by. These core values are: Transformational Change, Team, Leadership, Respect and Humility, and Diversity. My personal and professional values most certainly align with TFA's. I find all five of these values to be important. I would not join an organization if my values did not align with theirs.

■ *How do I reconcile differences between my values and those of my organization? How will these differences impact my ability to develop toward my vision and goals?*

Although I am not experiencing this currently, I imagine down the road I will find an organization where our values do not align perfectly. In that case, I will do what I always do: focus on the positive. What do I believe and how do I see that every day? I hope to be the type of person to challenge the organization and ask questions about the values or pieces I do not understand to gain insight and clarity. In an extreme case, perhaps my goals will change as I adapt new beliefs and values, or learn that the organization is simply not right for me.

## How do we do this?

■ *Who gives me feedback on their perspective of my progress? How often? What form would I like this feedback to take?*

Throughout my life, many people have provided me with feedback on my changes, my progress, and the things I have done. Family, professors, friends, and peers are the short list from whom I've heard about my progress. My mom and my brother give me the most feedback with regard to all aspects of my life; they are the people who know me best and have known me the longest, so naturally they will be the ones to offer the greatest and most impactful feedback. There is, indeed, a balance of when to give or expect to get feedback on progress. I am the type of person who likes a one-on-one conversation to receive feedback. The intimacy of a personal conversation makes me take the feedback more seriously and I am given the opportunity to ask questions and communicate any thoughts or ideas I may have to contribute.

■■■■■■

## Case Study: Kelly

*Kelly is an international student from China studying at The Ohio State University. As of this writing she is a college senior. You will learn more about her in the following case study.*

**Step 1: Create a picture of your future.** *Imagine yourself at the end of your life. You are looking back and imagining what you have done and the results you have created.*

■ *What is the thing of which you are most proud?*

I became a successful fashion merchandiser, I had my own retail stores that sold top luxury products selected from all over the world, and I had a loving family. I had both a successful professional career and family life. My work ethic made me financially independent and I chose the hours I worked. I only worked by appointment and invitation so that I had more time to do things I loved. I have a healthy body that enabled me to travel around to wonderful places with my friends and family.

■ *If you had a family, what would they say about you?*

I would like to imagine that my family would say about me what I say about my mother: she has a strong mind within her small body, she loves her family, and always prioritizes it in every situation, at the same time she is a professional role model because she is a successful executive in the banking industry. I want to be a great person, successful woman, and take great care of my family, like her.

■ *What did you accomplish professionally?*

I was at the top level of a company, managing many teams and in charge of marketing and communication. As an innovative leader, I brought my company to the next level of business and led it to be a highly reputable company, like *Vogue* magazine or Neiman Marcus, in the fashion industry. I had many social activities in which I met with celebrities and upper class people. These individuals appeared in my advertisements as models or spokespeople of my brand and products, and helped build my company's reputation and my own.

■ *What would your friends say about you?*

My friends would say that I was interesting in private settings and had fun stories that kept us talking all the time; I was a party host and conversation starter. Also, they respected me as a successful person. They were proud of me because I grew into a mature lady and had a good life that many people want. While I was successful, I was helpful and kind to them.

*For the rest of this exercise, let that future person speak to you and help you set a path that will enable you to look back with pride and say things like, "I feel fulfilled and at peace. I lived my life well."*

**Step 2: Write a story.** *Now that you have that image of what you will accomplish, write a brief story about your successful life. Include details about the questions above. Make it a story of what you went through to accomplish each of the results for the questions you answered. What you are trying to create is a roadmap for your journey that gives you more insight into what you would want if you had the option to design your perfect life.*

■ *Who helped you along the way?*

In the first twenty years of my life, my family helped me the most, in both my education and my career. They were like a lifelong school that taught me more than anyone else could.

I got support from my friends, coworkers, bosses, and even competitors. People who loved and respected me gave me the power and courage to fight for a better future. They not only supported me emotionally, but also provided sources to help me in different aspects of life, such as my relationships and career. I am thankful for people who compete with me or even dislike me. Competition kept me humble and seeking constant improvement. As I progressed through my life, I realized that help shifted from my parents and siblings to my husband and the friends I made at work and in the community. I developed strong friends in school and I stayed in touch with them over the years because the experiences we had studying abroad shaped our lives in a very important way. People who did not travel could not relate in the same way as people who left home early and had to deal with the challenges of living far from home and living abroad.

■ *What did you enjoy about your daily life?*

I was an optimistic person, although sometimes I was overwhelmed, so I built strong resilience that helped me get through adversity. As I look back on my life I realize the optimism I feel now carried me through my life. I continued to focus on resilience in my life because I continued to take on challenges that caused me stress. My belief that there was always a solution to any problem was also helpful. When others got frustrated and quit, my optimism, resilience, and problem-solving abilities allowed me to accomplish my goals and fulfill my vision.

My optimistic personality allowed me to regain happiness through very simple things, such as a nice piece of clothing, delicious food, or a kind message, so I was generally in a good mood. I continued to appreciate the little things in life. This allowed me to easily enjoy every day. When I was in a good mood, I was most productive, so this is part of what fueled my success and set me apart from other workers who are less productive and more moody.

### ◼ Who was closest to you?

Early after graduation, classmates, friends, and my boyfriend were my main support. I wasn't lonely as an international student. My friends and boyfriend brought me the feeling of home while I was away from my family. This ability to find a friend anywhere in the world has been a strong asset for me during my life. I developed an ability to navigate difficult situations that others did not develop so early. Later in life I married, and my husband and family became the people closest to me. I also maintained lifelong friendships with people I met in college and during my career.

### ◼ What feelings did you have as you accomplished each milestone along the way?

I was enthusiastic, constantly working toward each milestone. But after every milestone, I stopped for a while to calm down, looked back at what I did, summarized what I should not do, and what I should continue and improve. It helped me to know how to start another journey better, faster, and more efficiently. Because I was a positive person, I was able to celebrate my ongoing success and also put mistakes into perspective. I understood that if I was aggressively pursuing high goals, I made plenty of mistakes along the way and generally learned from each without letting myself get sidetracked.

### ◼ How did you mentor others and contribute to the success of others?

I have found mentoring has been important to me during college. As I look back on my life, I continued this trend of mentoring through my career. I made a practice of being open to people who came to me seeking my guidance and I also sought out people who I thought were promising to spend time with. This included people within my organization or other employees working abroad who could benefit from what I learned about navigating education in a foreign country.

### ◼ What did you do to maintain your health?

I exercised on the weekends or when I was free. I did my best to stay away from junk food. I loved laughing. I found that I continued to watch TV shows and movies, and read comics to release my stress and keep me mentally healthy. Being physically and mentally healthy made me highly productive.

I also had a reflection process that allowed me to focus on my goals daily and also evaluate my progress on a regular basis. I realized that when we keep our goals clearly in our minds, we are more likely to accomplish them.

■ *What role did spirituality or religion play in your journey?*

I am not a believer of any religion. I believe in myself. This is an important power that motivates me—how can you succeed if you don't even have faith in yourself? During the course of my life I found people with similar views about religion and we supported one another in our lives. We were all pretty self-reliant so we enjoyed taking on projects together and talking about the challenges we faced.

■ *What job did you have?*

I worked in different industries: animation/filmmaking, food, insurance, fashion, and electronics. People kept saying that I should settle down in one industry in order to go deeper and be more professional in a specific area. I never thought that way. During life, I pursued every chance trying out different industries to gain different experiences. This became a defining quality in my life—my sense of openness to new geographies, jobs, and ideas. Ultimately, my favorite work was within the fashion industry and it was where I spent much of my career after exploring different options.

Building on my habit of gaining broad experience, I held many jobs within the industry which helped me reach my long-term goal of being a successful marketing executive in the fashion industry.

■ *What role did material success play in your life?*

It was important for me. I think practically. I have always believed that material success built the base of my life. If you don't have a firm and strong base, how can you build on top of it? It is a resource, essential to maintaining your family, career, and needs. I obtained enough material success that I was ultimately able to focus on other dreams. I earned that success through hard work and dedication.

■ *What type of person were you (kind, caring, driven, and gracious)?*

I was a creative, gracious, caring, and motivated person. Whether with friends or with coworkers, I heard them saying "we trust you." This is one achievement that I am very proud of.

**Step 3: Describe your personal vision.** *Given the story you have written and the qualities you demonstrated as a person, write a two to five sentence life-purpose statement—a statement that talks about your highest priorities in life and your aspirations. This statement should capture the essence of how you want to live your life and project yourself.*

My highest priority in my life is always my family and friends, no matter what. While taking care of my family, I'm not giving up on my dream. I will always remember my life goals, which drive me to be stronger. So far, I am an ambitious college student and I want to show my creativity, ability, and value to other people. Although time may change my mind and goal, it won't change my passion for life. Finally, my passion will lead me to my dream career, being a successful marketing professional in the fashion industry, with a rich economic base to support my family.

**Step 4: Expand and clarify your vision.** *If you are like most people, the choices you wrote are a mixture of selfless and self-centered elements. People sometimes ask, "Is it all right to want to be covered in jewels, or to own a luxury car?" Part of the purpose of this exercise is to suspend your judgment about what is "worth" desiring, and to ask instead which aspect of these visions is closest to your deepest desire.*

*To find out, ask yourself the following questions about each element before going on to the next one: If I could have it now, would I take it? Some elements of your vision don't make it past this question. Others pass the test conditionally: "Yes, I want it, but only if…" Others pass, but are later clarified and distilled in the process. As you complete this exercise, refine your vision to reflect any changes you want to make.*

*After defining and clarifying your vision, it is time to consider your personal values. The combination of these two exercises will help you create the foundation of what you want to accomplish and the core principles that guide your actions as you work toward your vision.*

I will focus now on opportunities to fulfill and develop myself. I said what I care most about is my family and friends and I will structure my life so I can remain true to that priority. Additionally, I will achieve material success—new clothes for every season, jewels, shoes, and attend fashion shows. I will build a successful career in a fashion company and a loving family—all by upgrading my skills set and strengthening my personality to face all the difficulties along the way. I won't regret the choices I make. The life I choose will keep me motivated.

## *Kelly's Checklist for Personal Values*

Values are deeply held views of what we find worthwhile. They come from many sources: parents, religion, schools, peers, people we admire, and culture. Many go back to childhood; others are taken on as adults. Values help us define how we live our lives and accomplish our purpose.

**Step 1: Define what you value most.** From the list of values (both work and personal), select the ten that are most important to you—as guides for how to behave, or as components of a valued way of life. Feel free to add any values of your own to this list.

achievement, arts, self-development, creativity, cooperation, efficiency, health, friendship, relationship, and trust

**Step 2: Elimination.** Now that you have identified ten values, imagine that you are only permitted to have five. Which five would you give up? Cross them off. Now cross off another two to bring your list down to three. The remaining three are:

self-development, relationship, health

**Step 3: Integration.** Take a look at the top three values on your list.

- *How would your life be different if those values were prominent and practiced?*

I should keep learning new things in order to develop myself to a higher level, corresponding to the rapidly changing world. While being professional and skillful, one important thing that can let people see me is through relationships. Without good relationships, no matter how good I am, no one would appreciate and respect me. Last but not least, I need a healthy body to make sure I have the energy and focus to achieve my goals. Those values will bring me to a higher level of career and life. Without them I am just stepping on the same point and never moving forward.

- *What does each value mean, exactly? What do you expect from yourself, even in difficult times?*

1. **Self-development.** Develop myself not only physically but also emotionally. Being a professional person means there will be a lot of challenges. To master those challenges and to avoid being overwhelmed, I need to keep improving myself just like electronic equipment needs to keep upgrading the system to a better version, a better me.

2. **Relationships.** Everyone needs connections to other people. In my life, the strongest of these connections are with my family. However, building relationships is a skill, a skill that is needed for getting more opportunities. Good relationships with people also keep me in a good mood.

3. **Health.** You can do nothing without it. Health is forever and the very basis of a person's success. Only with health you can enjoy your time with your family, hang out with friends, work efficiently, and travel anywhere. It is never possible for me to risk or abandon my health to achieve material success. We should first be responsible for ourselves, and then we are able to be responsible for others.

- *Does the personal vision you've outlined reflect those values? If not, should your personal vision be expanded? Again, if not, are you prepared and willing to reconsider those values?*

My personal vision is a brief introduction of my vision that includes almost all of my values. Deeply in my heart, I do want to achieve these values, and improve them step by step. My personal vision may change over time, depending on the different stages of my life. After I have reached a new stage, I'll reconsider my goal, my path, and my method to ensure efficiency and direction in the next stage.

- *Are you willing to create a life in which these values are paramount, and help an organization put those values into action? Which one item on the list do you care most about?*

Yes, relationships are most important to me. As I have said before, family is going to be the main priority in my life. Also, building professional relationships will help me jumpstart my career.

*Putting Vision into Action Exercise*

**Step 1: Identify your foundation.** Answer the three questions below by compiling a list of responses to each.

- *What are you passionate about?*

  I really enjoy my school life right now. I have student organizations I'm active in, I'm in a group of people who study together, I have holidays/vacations that I can spend doing what I love. So, I guess I am passionate about my relationships with others and learning.

- *What meets your economic needs?*

  My economic needs now are supported by my parents, and partially by myself working a part-time job at school. I will soon live on my own, and I will become a marketing professional to support myself. I want my parents to enjoy their retiring life without worrying about my finances. And I want to build a stable financial base for my future family.

- *What can you be great at?*

  I can be a great marketing employee within the fashion industry, being respected as an innovative leader. Also, I need to be a great daughter, great friend, with emphasis on my value of relationships. Being a diligent and creative worker is one of the many ways I can improve and promote myself.

*Note: your answers to these questions should reflect your values from the Personal Values Checklist.*

**Step 2: Review and identify overlap.** *Review your answers and identify the overlaps.*

When I reviewed my answers, I found that I had a heavy focus on creativity and self-development. Personally, they are some of the cores of performing well in my job, expressing my value, and being an innovative leader. My emphasis on them aligns well with my passion.

**Step 3: Harvest the ideas.** *Based on the overlaps, do you see anything that might be incorporated in what you do or how you work? This could mean adding an additional skill or goal or allocating a portion of your study time to an activity that is aligned with your values.*

It seems that I put less effort in family relationship than friendship. It is maybe because I have been living far away from my family, who are still in China, since I was eighteen and came to the US alone. Over so many years I fought independently without my parents besides me. I got so independent that I occasionally ignore the importance of family. I currently strongly desire to have more time to spend with my family, listening to their advice for my studying, growth, and future. I should incorporate my creativity to develop a better family relationship. My parents gave me the gift of creativity; I should use it well to develop myself. I believe I should study more knowledge outside of academic textbooks to fulfill my life, and invest this knowledge into my creativity and other abilities.

## Kelly's Innovative Leadership Reflection Questions

### What do I think/believe?

■ *How do I see myself in the future? What trends do I see around me that impact this view? Have I considered how these trends impact the way I want to contribute?*

I always have a picture in my mind that I will be a successful marketing professional in the fashion retail industry. In time, I will settle back to China where my family is. From many international students I know, when I asked them where they want to be after graduation, most of them confessed that they eventually would want to go back to their home country because that is the place they feel most comfortable. I admit that this idea impacts me and makes me think in the same way. If they all go home, eventually most of my friends and my network will be there. Going back to my homeland, staying close to family, and continuing developing my career is the picture that I want to draw.

■ *After doing the exercise, what is my vision?*

After completing the exercise, I get a better sense of who I am currently and how to improve myself and prepare to be a leader. I emphasized the importance of certainty about myself many times because, according to Chapter 1, I know the basic step of being an innovative leader is to know yourself and your skill well. Knowing what you are good at and what you are not enough at, I started to look into myself. My vision of who I am and who I want to be is clearer than ever. My updated vision after completing the exercises is:

> My highest priority in my life is always my family and friends. I will build on my values of self-development, relationships, and health to become a successful marketing executive within the fashion industry, with a rich economic base to support my family.

### What do I do?

■ *What do I tell others about my vision? Do I have an "elevator speech"? Is it something I think is inspirational?*

When I tell people about my vision I talk both about my values and also my desire to be successful in the fashion industry. I may be more experienced than other college students as I've had internships every summer since freshman year. Actually sometimes my friends ask me how to find an internship and how we should perform. I shared my experience and explained my vision to them, and I hope that my story can inspire them.

■ *How do I synthesize competing goals and commitments to create a vision that works for me in the context of the communities I serve?*

If my goals were competing or conflicting, I would consider which is more valuable to me at the current stage of my life and career. Then, I will achieve whichever is more valuable. In the context of the communities, finding balance is essential. I will never go extreme on any one of them and ignore the others. Understanding what I want is the key to finding the balance. After clearly knowing what I want, I will leverage other elements that may conflict with it and try to balance them. I realize that when I return to China I will be living in a different environment than I do now, and I will be faced with different choices.

## What do we believe?

■ *How does my personal vision fit within the larger context of my family, my community, my industry, or my job?*

My personal vision fits well within the context of my family, community, education, and job. As a daughter, being creative and responsible to bringing happiness to the whole family is important, and is the best way to pay back your family. While studying at school, to develop certain skills, for example leadership, I joined student organizations. Being a marketing member doing all the advertising jobs for the organization, my ability and my value is affirmed by my teammates. Sometimes the knowledge I learn from a book is not applicable or useful in the real world because the world changes every second. Therefore, thanks to student organization activities, I built an updated base of professional skills and leadership. Once I find a chance to practice a certain skill in a real corporate environment, I will bring my passion and other skills to that environment. As for my community, I share similar values and vision with many members of my community.

## How do we do this?

■ *How do I monitor the organization's impact on my vision? How do I honor my vision when helping define/refine the organizational vision?*

I keep a monthly summary of my work progress and my development. From these summaries, I can easily monitor the impact of the company's culture and value. For example, I found out that I learned a lot from my supervisors, and my working pattern and method become more and more like theirs. Especially after a long interview with my supervisor about his career path, I found that the company's values impact him as well, and then he impacts me with his values. I honor my vision by seeing where it matches with the company's vision—we are young, ambitious, creative, and crave innovation. I am happy to work in a company with values and goals that motivate me.

■ *Who gives me feedback on their perspective of my progress? How often? What form would I like this feedback to take?*

I get feedback from anyone I work with, not only my supervisors, but other coworkers. I have a lot of communication with them in order to understand each other's ideas to do the projects better. During the communication, I hear them teaching and evaluating my work. Such kind of direct, face-to-face feedback is the clearest and easiest way to exchange thoughts. It helps me to identify the best way to do the project and to improve myself.

### ■ *Your Process of Creating a Compelling Vision*

Now that you have read Anthony's, Kelly's, and Shelby's personal narratives, it is time to complete the exercises and answer the questions for yourself. We encourage you to complete all of the exercises. These exercises establish a strong foundation for your personal vision, values, and course of action, so exercise patience and give yourself time to explore your hopes and dreams as authentically as possible. You will know you've completed this step and are ready to move to the next when you feel you have created a vision and set of values that truly inspire you.

Throughout this chapter, we have discussed exercises that will help you clarify your life direction and create a compelling vision for your own life and work. The next chapter focuses on assessing where you are right now in your career and personal development.

## Define personal vision and values

## What do I think/believe?

## What do I do?

**What do we believe?**

**How do we do this?**

# CHAPTER 3

## Step 2: Analyze Your Situation and Strengths

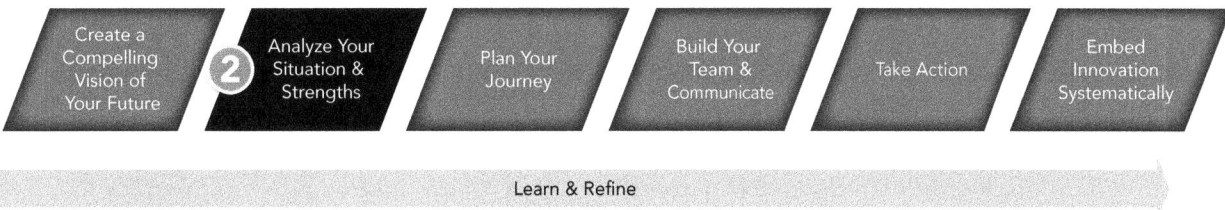

Now that you have developed your vision, this step will help you examine, refine, and clarify your strengths and growth opportunities using standard assessment tools. You will then decide which areas you would like to improve by building on what you already do well and managing your weaknesses. We recommend using a general guideline that focuses eighty percent of your effort on building your existing strengths and twenty percent on addressing weaker areas. Though this is a general approximation, the 80/20 rule is a directional one stemming from the belief that you are more successful when you focus on building your strengths rather than improving your weaknesses.

### *Future Projections*

As you think about your strengths and weaknesses it will be important to think about your future career direction and the trends in that industry. Because the world is changing so quickly, you will benefit from building skills and focusing your development in an area that is growing. An example of growing industries right now is big data and analytics. As an emerging field, there is a shortage of people trained to fill these jobs. Next year, job trends will change so keeping current will help you shape your direction.

It is also important to consider your true passions and interests as they align with your strengths. What do you enjoy doing outside of school work? In which classes are you motivated to do the reading simply because you enjoy it? When talking with your classmates and peers about current issues, what topics are you most passionate about? These types of questions can help lead you to considering how you might apply your strengths to a future job or career.

We also find that reading futurist publications in specific industries is helpful. The role of the futurist is to evaluate current trends and build possible scenarios for how the future might unfold. By building on our capacities for leadership, we can use these scenarios as part of our planning process to provide insight into overall societal trends, ensure that we are well prepared for the potential impact of ever-changing business conditions, and suggest imminent scenarios that help to navigate those trends effectively.

There are several organizations providing very effective views into the future. One that we regularly reference is The Arlington Institute (TAI) founded in 1989 by futurist John L. Petersen. It is a nonprofit research institute that specializes in thinking about global futures and creating conditions to influence rapid, positive change. They encourage systemic, nonlinear approaches to planning and believe that effective thinking about the future is enhanced by applying emerging technology. TAI strives to be an effective agent of advancement by creating intellectual frameworks and toolsets for understanding the transitional times in which we are living that are marked by significant and ongoing changes across industry and sector.

It is important to combine your vision with a firm understanding of your current strengths, capacities, and resources. The data will help you become more aware of your opportunities for growth, and also clarify how others see you. This combination of information will help you determine the gap between your current state (based on assessment data) and your vision.

When you begin taking assessments, it will be important to get information from a broad range of sources to ensure you have a clear and accurate picture of your true capacity, as well as to understand how others see you, and to clarify how you see yourself. It is also important to reflect deeply on the results you receive. Some results will resonate with you and some will not. These tools are helpful for personal growth and as a starting point for evaluating your behavior and goals. However, these tools do not substitute for solid personal investment in self-reflection. Combined, both the assessment tools and the time you spend reflecting on your own emotions, reactions, and behaviors can lead to a greater understanding of yourself and how you interact with others.

Leadership Behaviors

Situational Analysis

Resilience

Leadership Maturity

Leader Type

## Assessment Tools

One of the primary ways to help you understand your current development and performance is by using a combination of assessments to measure your current skills and abilities, along with your personality style and developmental perspective. This should allow you to identify the gap between your present state and what you need to fulfill your vision.

There are several good assessments available. The tools we suggest have been used extensively with our students and we recommend them with a high degree of confidence. We find that each provides vital information in helping to convey a comprehensive picture of strengths, weaknesses, and opportunities. These assessments are aligned with the five leadership elements discussed in Chapter One. The Metcalf & Associates free online assessment does not replace the detailed assessments recommended below, but does offer a high-level view of your innovative leadership and can indicate key areas of focus. It can be accessed by going to www.metcalf-associates.com/innovative-leadership-assessment.

*The tools we use to help develop emerging innovative leaders are:*

■ **Innovative Leadership Assessment (found at the beginning of this workbook)**

This short self-assessment helps you identify your own scores relating to Innovative Leadership for university students. It is organized by the five domains of Innovative Leadership. This will give you a general sense of where you want to focus your efforts. We encourage you to take this survey as a way to get a snapshot of where you excel and where you may want to focus your energies.

■ **Resilience Assessment**

Metcalf & Associates created a basic tool that helps you assess your attitudes and practices to support resilience, and to identify areas to further build your capacity. It is based on fundamental stress management research including the characteristics that support "stress hardiness," a concept pioneered by Suzanne Kobasa. This assessment can be found at www.metcalf-associates.com/resilience-assessment-tool.

■ **Emotionally Intelligent Leadership for Students Assessment**

This resource is a combination of two bodies of literature and research—emotional intelligence and leadership development. The book and assessment help you reflect on your scores across nineteen leadership capacities, and help you improve your ability to view your natural tendencies and behaviors through the lenses of your interactions with others, your environment, and how you view yourself.

You can purchase the *Emotionally Intelligent Leadership: A Guide for Students* and the assessment through any bookstore or online. Be sure to select the newest version (the 2nd edition) of both. This is currently only available as a self-scoring paper assessment, but does a great job of walking you through the self-scoring process and provides charts and helpful information related to your results. Then, when you read the book, you can think critically about how to capitalize on your top capacities of emotionally intelligent leadership and which capacities you need to explore further for improvement.

■ **Competency Assessment**

Understanding your strengths is the first step to greater self-awareness, and a better understanding of how to capitalize on your natural talents and abilities. Grounded in Positive Psychology, strengths-based approaches provide leaders with important perspectives of working in teams and groups, and the tools to engage in meaningful, positive application of their personal strengths. By learning how to capitalize on their own individual strengths and the strengths of others, emerging leaders learn the importance of building a diverse team, appreciating the contributions of team members, and the art of delegating for overall team success.

Based on the culmination of more than fifty years of Dr. Donald O. Clifton's lifelong work, we recommend *StrengthsFinder,* an assessment that has led millions of people around the world to discover their strengths. According to the latest research by the Gallup Organization, the thirty-four *StrengthsFinder* themes naturally cluster into four domains of leadership strength. The assessment identifies your top five themes and sorts them into the four domains (executing, influencing, relationship building, and strategic thinking). This information is very helpful as you think about how you can contribute to a team and how to partner effectively with others.

You have two options for taking the *StrengthsFinder* assessment.

1) You can take it through the StrengthsQuest program designed especially for applying strengths in the collegiate setting. Visit the strengthsquest.com website and click on the link to "purchase" an online code. Once you complete the assessment online, you will have access to resources on the StrengthsQuest website that specifically connect your strengths to your academics, career planning, co-curricular activities, and to student leadership.

2) You can purchase the book titled, *Strengths-Based Leadership* and then use the code in the back of the book to take the online assessment. This version provides you with the specific tools for using your strengths in leadership settings. You can find the book in bookstores or online. Just be sure to purchase a new version of the book so the code to take the online assessment included with the book is unused.

Both options are good. It just depends on how you plan to utilize your strengths. To maximize your knowledge of strengths, you could purchase a code via StrengthsQuest to take the assessment and then purchase a used copy of the Strengths-Based Leadership book to apply your strengths to leadership in organizational settings. We use the Strengths-Based Leadership book in our classes with students because we feel that the content is valuable.

Because this assessment is based in Positive Psychology, it will help you see your strengths more clearly and it will challenge you to view leadership from this new paradigm of appreciation. This provides you a solid foundation to build upon. By design, however, it does not provide insight into your weaknesses. Strengths-based approaches to leadership support the philosophy that you should FOCUS on your strengths and MANAGE your weaknesses. The better way to handle weakness is to surround yourself with people who are naturally talented in the areas where you are lacking in strength, or to capitalize on your strengths when you encounter stumbling blocks along the way. It is also recommended that you ensure your leadership role does not require that you operate from an area of lesser strength the majority of the time. Research on strengths has shown that the highest achievers in a variety of fields: (1) operate the majority of the time from an area of strength; (2) have learned to partner or delegate to compensate for areas that are not their strength; (3) capitalize on their strengths in new situations; and (4) use their strengths to overcome obstacles (Rath and Conchie, 2008).

It can be helpful to take multiple assessments during the same period of time to paint a more complete and accurate picture of who you are as a leader. For example, *StrengthsFinder* shows your strengths and the *Emotionally Intelligent Leadership for Students: Inventory* evaluates your leader capacities from the lenses of self, others, and environment. The combined or integrated assessments allow you to better understand your innate skills and abilities as well as your opportunities. This comprehensive information allows you to determine how you fit within your organization or within a future career. Keep in mind that interpreting the data from these and other assessments may require specialized expertise; we recommend you seek out opportunities to take these assessments, or similar ones, with the help of leadership educators, faculty, or career counselors when this support is available. If support is not available, it is important that you develop a clear understanding of what the assessment tells you so you can benefit from it. Another healthy practice is to share your results with friends, family, or colleagues who know you well. Ask them to reflect on your results and give you examples of when they have seen those behaviors, emotions, or capacities exhibited from you. This can be excellent feedback and support for your development process.

Out of the four different types of assessments presented to you, take the opportunity to select the ones you are moved to take and consider how best to utilize the results.

### Tools and Exercises

Now that you have reviewed the tools and taken some or all of the assessments, it is time to synthesize what you have learned about yourself through a Strengths, Weaknesses, Opportunities, and Threats worksheet (SWOT), and through a series of reflection questions. For the SWOT analysis, please complete the worksheet below.

| TABLE 3.1: SWOT ANALYSIS | |
|---|---|
| **Strengths**<br><br>*What sets you apart from most other people?* | **Opportunities**<br><br>*What opportunities are open to those who have these strengths?* |
| **Weaknesses**<br><br>*What do you need to improve?* | **Threats**<br><br>*Do you have weaknesses that need to be addressed before you can move forward?* |

## *Development Journey Continued*

Anthony, Shelby, and Kelly will now walk through their worksheets and journal entries for analyzing their individual situation and strengths.

---

### ANTHONY'S SWOT WORKSHEET ANSWERS

### Strengths

#### What sets you apart from most other people?

One of my biggest strengths is the competitive edge I maintain over other people. My Gallup strength of competition drives me to succeed and forces me to stay abreast of others around me.

I also have achiever as a Gallup strength. I have a strong drive to achieve great things. Because of this, I have developed excellent preparation habits, an unrelenting work ethic to finish things I start, and an ability to raise my performance under pressure situations. I believe what truly sets me apart is the combination of competitive fire along with a cerebral and perceptive side. I am very introspective and I use my ability to analyze people and situations to map out future game plans in my head. This allows me to be an excellent director in teams. My ability to motivate people and bring tactical guidance to teams is a separating factor for me. I have a yearning to acquire new knowledge (my Gallup learner strength) and this helps me thrive in dynamic environments. I am also very positive and consistent in my approach to handling things.

### Opportunities

#### What opportunities are open to those who have these strengths?

My strengths and skillset translate well to the business world. I try very hard to make myself as well-rounded as possible in order to avail myself to all options. The best opportunities for someone with these strengths is as a manager or director of a team or organization. My demeanor will allow me to navigate through the ultra-competitive corporate world. There seem to be opportunities at the top of companies for people who are able to both analyze and motivate other workers. People who are highly aware of the world around them (high consciousness of context on the EIL assessment) are able to adapt and conquer in the corporate world.

I realize I will need to work my way up to use some of these skills while others make me a natural fit as a financial analyst.

### Weaknesses

#### What do you need to improve?

I need to control my competitiveness so that I can better *manage my personal relationships*. I crave being best at everything I do, and that desire can sometimes lead to negative feelings toward coworkers who I want to outperform. I never outwardly express or plot against my colleagues, but I am keenly aware that any failure they have results in an opportunity for me to shine. It is important that I place my personal relationships with people above my quest to outperform them. The finance industry is all about connections and trust. Building mutually beneficial relationships in which both parties trust each other is essential.

Another weakness I have is *overanalyzing things*. My Gallup strength of "analytical" often causes me to work on trivial tasks for more time than is actually needed. Prioritizing my tasks better would help me solve this problem. I also have a difficult time being proactive. When this weakness gets in my way, it can cause me to fall behind on projects and experience unnecessary stress as deadlines loom. It could also cause me to miss out on potential opportunities in my professional career.

### Threats

#### Do you have weaknesses that need to be addressed before you can move forward? Do any weaknesses pose an immediate threat, such as losing your job?

I would like to address my ability to *prioritizing my career progress and my relationships*. I can sometimes get caught up in my career goals when I should be more concerned with the personal relationships I develop along the way. This includes how my sometimes overpowering need to compete and win may impact a relationship. I realize that to succeed, I need to be more of a team player and I cannot do this when I am trying to outshine everyone around me.

Before moving forward, I need to address my inability to finish tasks that are assigned without a timetable. If a deadline is not firmly laid out, I often struggle with procrastination. This weakness is amplified when I perceive the task to be trivial. Another reason for my issue with procrastination may be my tendency to overanalyze situations. This causes me to lose time on small tasks which could otherwise be diverted to more important responsibilities. I should also be less concerned with the way people see me. I often put too much pressure on myself to please others.

## SHELBY'S SWOT WORKSHEET ANSWERS

### Strengths

**What sets you apart from most other people?**

My ability to combine my strengths and use them concurrently sets me apart. My top strengths are Maximizer, Woo, Positivity, Developer, and Communication. I use Communication the most, especially since it is one of my majors. Not only am I able to write a killer essay about Hamlet, but also I can prepare and perform a speech in front of thousands of people without batting an eyelash. I am able to combine my strength in Communication with Positivity when I need to motivate someone or when mentoring. I put Communication and Woo together with a big smile and a firm handshake when I need people to like and want me, for example in job interviews. I believe my most dominant strength is Positivity. People like happy, lively people. That's what I am and that is what sets me apart from others.

### Opportunities

**What opportunities are open to those who have these strengths?**

Someone who can speak and write well is someone to be reckoned with. "Communicators" can get our points across concisely, write a beautiful poem, chat with the Starbucks barista, or tell a story with zeal and confidence. Public speaking does not daunt "the Communicator." We can get in front of a crowd of 100 to 10,000 and speak.

Being an excellent and confident communicator opens doors for many different professions and careers. I believe a huge part of why I was hired for Teach for America so early (spring of my junior year in college) is because I interviewed well and communicated exactly what they needed to hear from me in an efficient way. Companies want people with strong communication skills. Other skills can be taught or learned, but being a natural communicator is an innate strength.

### Weaknesses

**What do you need to improve?**

It has always been hard for me to have really great Strategic Thinking skills in day-to-day life. Unlike talking and writing, Strategic Thinking does not come naturally to me. I need to work on this especially in a work environment. I can get caught up in conversations and laughing during a meeting instead of going through the planned-out agenda.

I need to take this area of weakness and try more to infiltrate the fluff in my brain with more strategic ways of doing things, not just what will make people happy or "okay." I need to improve focusing less on feelings and more on thinking. A better balance will help my work ethic.

Additionally, I enjoy communicating so much that I often talk over people. I don't always allow them to finish speaking before I start to talk. I recognize that this is a characteristic that does not serve me well, and one that I need to improve.

### Threats

**Do you have weaknesses that need to be addressed before you can move forward?**

A weakness that would potentially pose a threat is that I am very stubborn. When I think, feel, believe something, I REALLY think, feel, and believe it. And I am not easily swayed from my own perspective. If I think if I am not open to additional perspectives and become a better listener, my stubbornness could get in the way of my job.

## KELLY'S SWOT WORKSHEET ANSWERS

### Strengths

**What sets you apart from most other people?**

My top five strengths are:

1. Communication

2. Strategic

3. Individualization

4. Woo (winning others over)

5. Positivity

My strengths help me on many things—projects, personal interactions, and daily life. I believe that I have found a good balance between relationship building and strategic thinking. I use my strengths of Woo and Positivity to relate to people in my internship and seek out mentors. I am able to positively influence those around me while also focusing on the best way to get to a goal (strategic).

### Opportunities

**What opportunities are open to those who have these strengths?**

I believe that almost every job requires these strengths. I am capable of creativity and innovation, and my strength of individualization helps me to personalize designs and ideas to the individual needs of a person or a company. My strategic strength will be useful in all my work. It allows me to take time to assess risk, avoid the less-beneficial opportunities, and navigate toward the best options. I am able to assess situations efficiently and carefully before moving forward. This will help me in my career and in my own self-development.

### Weaknesses

**What do you need to improve?**

I need to be more vocal about my ideas and aggressive toward my goals. I can use my strengths of strategic and communication to improve in this area. Before I started working in a company, I only worked in a café on campus. I thought that what I learned in class was really what we would do in the real world. After my first professional internship, my thoughts totally changed. I realized that to succeed, I need to work on skills I can't learn in the classroom like being confident enough to speak up and network. I have the communication strength which shows in my writing—I just need to develop the courage to use it verbally with peers, faculty members, and colleagues. I also need to gain experience in the fashion industry because none of my internships have been fashion related.

### Threats

**Do you have weaknesses that need to be addressed before you can move forward? Do any pose an immediate threat like losing your job?**

I would like to address my ability to be more active in groups. During meetings, I sometimes come up with ideas that I think may be valuable, but I never speak up. This is one of my biggest weaknesses, especially in front of people who are on a higher level than me. When I say an idea aloud, I find that my coworkers do consider my ideas or questions valuable. I realize that as a new person in the workplace, one way to draw people's attention—and show my ability—is to talk. And since I have a strength of communication, I just need to capitalize on it.

My lack of fashion experience could keep me from working in my dream area. It won't keep me from getting a job. But I do think that if I don't gain experience, I will not be able to get a good job in the fashion industry and move up like I want to.

## *Innovative Leadership Reflection Questions*

To help you develop your action plan, it is time to further clarify your direction using reflection questions. The questions for "What do I think/believe?" reflect your intentions. "What do I do?" questions reflect your actions. The questions "What do we believe?" reflect the culture of your organization (i.e., work, school, community), and "How do we do this?" questions reflect systems and processes for your organization. This exercise is an opportunity to practice innovative leadership by considering your vision for yourself and how it will play out in the context of your life. You will define your intentions, actions, culture, and systems in a systematic manner.

Table 3.2 contains an exhaustive list of questions to appeal to a broad range of readers. Find a few that fit your own personal situation; focus on the questions that seem the most relevant. We recommend you answer one to three questions from each category.

## *Real World Application*

### Personal Cheat Sheet

After viewing the results of all your assessments, create a document that has a summary of each assessment result. This will work as your personal "cheat sheet," or master document, for your skills and leadership development. If you are ever uncertain about how to best utilize your strengths in an individual or group setting, refer to this cheat sheet. Also, the very process of creating this cheat sheet requires you to closely analyze and study your assessment results and record them briefly in your own words, thus giving you a greater understanding of your situation. You can also infuse your personal creativity into this process. Make this document, chart, or picture something that you can refer to easily and access an understanding of where your results intersect. I once had a student create a "road map" of assessment results—intersecting roads were places where she saw similarities in her results and they "intersected," while stoplights were representative of when her results got in her way or stopped her from achieving her goals. On ramps and off ramps led her to certain goals using particular aspects of her assessment results.

Write using bullet-points or pictures and symbols instead of a paragraph format; in this way it is easier to find specific pieces of information. Try to make a few high-quality points for each section. It doesn't have to be a long document, but it will be critical to your success in achieving your goals and becoming an innovative leader.

## TABLE 3.2: REFLECTION QUESTIONS

**What do I think/believe?**

- Given the direction the world is evolving, how are you positioned to be a leader in the future?

- Are you able to balance academic, professional, and personal commitments? How has your current leadership style contributed to the organization's success? Have you done things that did not produce the results you had hoped for? How would you change to produce different results?

- How would you like to impact the people who work with you? Have they grown and met their goals while working with you? What have they contributed to the organization while working with you?

- If you are leading a change initiative, what will you need to change to lead this effort effectively? Will you lead the same way this time, or will you change from what you have done in the past?

**What do I do?**

- How do you play to your strengths?

- How do you mitigate the threats?

- How do you take advantage of opportunities?

- How do you compensate for weaknesses?

- What other assessments are you taking to gather objective data about your performance? This could include performance appraisals, developmental assessments, 360° feedback, or informal feedback from multiple sources.

- How do you appropriately respond to your personal sense of urgency while supporting organizational objectives?

- What messages do you convey that use emotion, external expert sources, and sense of clarity to demonstrate urgency?

- How do you communicate your personal changes and your sense of urgency to those around you who may be impacted?

**What do we believe?**

- Notice the various people and groups in your life (family, colleagues, boss, community, friends, etc.); what do they consider "urgent"?

- Anticipate how they will interpret your change. How will they talk about it? Specifically, for your organization, how will the changes you aspire to make impact others?

- Determine how your sense of urgency connects with the group's sense of urgency based on its priorities, goals, and pain points.

- How does the culture of your support system impact your beliefs about yourself and about leadership? Would these beliefs change if you changed who you spent time with?

- Based on developmental perspectives, where is the cultural center of gravity in your support system? How are people with more open perspectives perceived?

- What are the cultural barriers impeding your changes? What are the cultural enablers? Will your changes be aligned with the organizational culture? Will they send a message that you do not value the culture?

> **How do we do this?**
>
> - What groups or programs are enablers or barriers that may impact my development?
> - What processes and measures alert you to urgency in your system that we need to tend to? What are the early warning signs?
> - What processes measure your progress? Are you progressing as measured by criteria that will increase your professional effectiveness? Are you progressing based on your personal standards? How will your support system or organization reward or punish your changes based on the measures?
> - Do the measures indicate a sense of urgency to you that support focusing on your development?

## Development Journey Continued

Anthony, Shelby, and Kelly will now walk through their reflection questions and journal entries for analyzing their individual situation and strengths.

### Anthony's Responses

### What do I think/believe?

- **Are you able to balance business and personal commitments? How does your leadership style impact your ability to meet your overall life goals?**

I believe that I do a very good job at balancing personal commitment with school. Being a college baseball player means that your time for schoolwork gets cut in half. It means that early mornings and late nights are sometimes necessary to complete all of my classwork. I like to plan out my days by writing down what I have to do so I can check it off after I completed it. One of my strengths on the *StrengthsFinder* assessment was "achiever" and the description discusses this list-making strategy. Being able to cross items off my list is a great feeling for me because of the time that I balanced to get that task done. While I am still developing my true leadership style I believe that my ability to make others feel comfortable in their roles and having a positive attitude was part of my role as a senior on the baseball team. I believe leaders work for others while guiding them to be the best they can be. My life goals of having a great job and family life will be impacted by my abilities to find the positives in others and helping them to be their best.

- **How has your leadership style contributed to the organization's success? Have you done things that did not produce the results you had hoped for? How would you change to produce different results?**

My hard work, dedication, and time management have contributed to my college success. I remember being a freshman and most everything in my life was new to me and somewhat uncomfortable. Given my time commitments of balancing classes and baseball, I may have focused on the sports aspects more in freshman year than I should have. I am very hard on myself and I am never satisfied with my performance (probably a result of my competition strength), which is why results from freshman year were not what I would have hoped for in baseball or class work. I should have spent more time balancing my time after practice to get ahead in my classes instead of watching television or hanging out with teammates.

## What do I do?

■ *How do you compensate for weaknesses?*

One of the ways I compensate for my weaknesses is by playing to my strengths. If I am faced with a problem in college, at my internship/job, or in everyday life then I think of how my five strengths can help me to achieve success. I try always to learn from every mistake and to make decisions that will not lead me to another similar mistake. Leadership is all about finding a person's strengths and having that person participate in tasks that they are strongest at. I do not look at compensating for my weaknesses as much as knowing my strengths and using them to the best of my ability. My strengths are based on experiences and are innate parts of my behavior that I should capitalize on whenever I can. I also value other people's opinions. Seeking information from others on how they handled a problem, or researching a topic or process using my learner strength, helps compensate for weaknesses.

■ *How do you take advantage of opportunities?*

I have learned from my mistakes. I like to weigh the positives and negatives of each opportunity. I actually will make a pro and con list for big decisions to try and help guide my decision. Every challenge presents an opportunity to learn and grow either personally or professionally. The easiest thing that you can do in any opportunity is give it your all, never stop learning, and listen to good advice while learning everything from others who know more than you do. One of the things I truly believe is that you should never shy away from an opportunity even though it may make you uncomfortable. If I am honest with my assessment of an opportunity, and it points me in the direction of undertaking the project, then I look at it as an open door and walk through it.

## What do we believe?

■ *How does the culture of your support system impact your beliefs about yourself and about leadership? Would these beliefs change if you changed who you spent time with?*

I grew up in a household with two supportive and loving parents who worked hard for everything they had. I saw my parents as strong people—as individuals and as a couple—and it greatly impacted my drive to be strong, and to be a leader. My father is the senior director of rehabilitation at a prestigious clinic in Ohio. When I was young, I watched him stop into his offices and interact with his staff. I saw that he was able to get the most out of his employees by truly caring about each one of them and by using humor. He helped them succeed by realizing and supporting their strengths. I learned that leadership is really serving others and not just telling people what to do when, where, and how. I also feel my support system taught me to treat everyone the same and always respect others. My mother is very involved in volunteering for projects in our community and church. Often we would help her at events, setting up, or cleaning up afterward and this taught me the importance of active involvement in my community. Our circle of friends growing up were of the same mindset and as involved as my family was, so I do believe that who you choose to be around has an impact. If I were to spend time with people who did not care about being involved and were what I call "takers," then I am sure some of their personality and behaviors would rub off on me. However, I believe your culture, traditions, and support system in your formative years define who you will be later in life. Keeping this in mind as we interact with others as leaders is important too. You don't know people's stories. So, the capacities outlined in the EIL assessment like empathy are very important to consider.

## How do we do this?

■ *What systems and processes are enablers or barriers that will impact my development?*

My development will be based on realizing that everyone and everything I encounter has a component of enabling and of being a barrier. An education has allowed me to progress. Teachers and professors in college are second only to family for interaction time in life. Having engaged, caring teachers who motivate each student in ways to maximize their potential is key to enabling successful development. In college, professors that demand the best from you are the ones you learn from the most—regardless of your final grade. Good teachers, and others you interact with in life, encourage the process of learning and developing. Interaction with professionals in the business world through internships, and family friends has helped me realize what it takes to be successful in business. Barriers are simply opportunities. Some system barriers that will impact my development are the economic and political climate in the country today. Companies are not hiring young graduates at the rate they were before. Setting myself apart by capitalizing on opportunities will be even more important today than it was in the past. A lack of experience is a barrier for new graduates trying to enter the work force. Taking advantage of and learning from each opportunity turns a barrier into a positive in my development. Time is an additional barrier to my development. Having enough minutes in the day to devote to both academics and athletics in college has been difficult. Time barriers force me to be very efficient and organized in completing projects, studying, and practicing.

■ *What processes and measures alert you to urgency in your system that we need to tend to? What are the early warning signs?*

Urgency in my personal system is affected by the ability to organize the processes of life. Having in place a clear "to do" prioritized list of what I need to accomplish makes it easier for me to meet my goals. Asking for feedback early and making adjustments as necessary in a project helps me stay on track with the process and with tasks. When new projects are added to my existing list, I have to take a moment and reprioritize the process of completing everything in a timely manner. My father taught me the 6 P's: Prior Proper Planning Prevents Poor Performance. I try to live by that as much as possible. When I feel overloaded I pay attention to the early warning signs that I have experienced that include a decrease in performance in one area of my life when I have had trouble meeting the urgency of a situation in another part of my life. An example of this would be allowing a poor performance on a test affect my performance in a baseball game that evening. Not balancing my focus to meet the demands of what is required to complete all goals and objectives creates stress. I believe stress is an early warning sign that I am not meeting urgent demands, or that I am falling behind in completing projects.

## Shelby's Responses

## What do I think/believe?

- **Are you able to balance business and personal commitments? How does your leadership style impact your ability to meet your overall life goals?**

My leadership style and my personality are a combination package. I lead with my heart and treat people with kindness and warmth. In a professional setting, I am positive, outgoing, and bubbly with coworkers and people in leadership roles. I keep my promises, make deadlines, and am very organized. On a personal level, I am friendly, excitable, and fun to be around because I love to try new things and especially love to laugh and have a good time. I see parallels between business and personal in that I wear a smile nearly everywhere I go and talk to everyone I'm around. (Yes, even strangers.) My perspective in the workplace and out in the world is Why not say hi? You like it when people smile or talk to you! This is obviously indicative of my strengths of positivity and communication.

I believe my leadership style is going to affect my ability to meet my overall life goals in a ridiculously positive way. I network and make friends sometimes without even knowing I'm doing it! I try to be memorable and remarkable when interacting with others. I want people to remember meeting me and have a happy, good feeling when they think of our encounter. I can utilize my strengths to leverage relationships into my career. My leadership style is warm and welcoming.

- **How has your leadership style contributed to the organization's success? Have you done things that did not produce the results you had hoped for? How would you change to produce different results?**

I believe my ability to model leadership to others has greatly contributed to the success I have seen. If I want e-mail returned in a timely fashion, I reply within twenty-four hours. If I want people to be friendly and confident, I show friendliness and confidence in my work. People long for someone to look up to and emulate. I do too; so, when I'm in a leadership position, I do what I can to be that person people look to model their leadership style after. Then, it's a strong leadership chain of hardworking, dedicated, passionate people who model the way for their followers and fellow leaders. In the EIL assessment, there was an emphasis on understanding context and environment. I think that role modeling is a big part of building a healthy environment.

Results do not happen when I'm not passionate about the work. It is extremely difficult for me to work on something I don't believe in or do not see value in, and I can't fake it. My capacity of "authenticity" on the EIL assessment can attest to this quality in me. To change this, I see importance in asking questions and gaining insight before tackling a task that seems like something maybe I'm not too keen on. Doing a bit of investigation beforehand can help me gain more perspective and perhaps prevent disengagement or disdain.

## What do I do?

### ◢ How do you compensate for weaknesses?

It has taken me a long time to learn how to compensate for weaknesses. The first step, honestly, was acknowledging my weaknesses and downfalls, which was difficult in itself! Once I was able to accept that (1) I have weaknesses, and (2) I can find ways to compensate, then I was able to move forward. My way of working through my weaknesses is relying on other people I trust and believe in to fill in my gaps. If I am really struggling with a project that involves technology I'm not used to doing and don't feel comfortable with, I will find a person to make it happen, or to show me how to do something. It is crucial to leadership development to learn how to swallow my pride and ask for help when I need it. That was one of my most difficult obstacles, but once I did it, I was able to make up for my weaknesses and empower others by utilizing their strengths.

### ◢ How do you take advantage of opportunities?

I jump on every opportunity I receive. Sometimes I don't even think, I just do. A lot of what I do and how I handle situations is through intuition; so, if an opportunity feels right, I'll more than likely say yes and go for it. I take advantage of opportunities by really living in the moments I experience. I try to feel everything deeply as I go through happiness, worry, stress, success, etc. Even with opportunities like two-hour-long volunteer projects, I try to experience its wonder and learn from where I am, what I'm doing, and who I'm with. Like the EIL assessment states, it is important to consider your own approach, but also to consider what you can learn from others in the process.

## What do we believe?

◼ **How does the culture of your support system impact your beliefs about yourself and about leadership? Would these beliefs change if you changed who you spent time with?**

Let go and let God were the words my mom used in almost every situation we were in growing up. My number one support system is my mom and my brother, followed by my hometown community. I come from a one-mile-long village in southeastern Ohio; it's a tight-knit farming community and I grew up thinking that everywhere was like my town. I knew everyone, I was comfortable, felt safe, and I pretty much liked everyone and everything, too. In college, I have found a way to get to know a lot of people and like a lot of people, too. I got to a place where I felt comfortable and safe. I have made my college experience like my hometown without even knowing it. My leadership style is welcoming and approachable, similar to the quaint, smallness of my hometown. I know if I would have grown up in another place with different people, I would be a different leader. I love that I can take the wonderful pieces of my hometown with me as I go and lead in different parts of Ohio and, perhaps, the world.

## How do we do this?

◼ **What systems and processes are enablers or barriers that will impact my development?**

My innate friendliness is certainly an enabler to my development. My college education and the success I have had in college will enable me to do more and be more in life. What I have learned through various involvements and jobs will certainly help me learn and grow at a faster rate in my next jobs and experiences.

Although I am aware and fully recognize my privileges in society based on my dominant identities, as a young, white, blonde, blue-eyed woman, I believe that—for all the opportunities privilege provides—in some cases there will be offsetting challenges. Being young is difficult because you are not always taken seriously or fully trusted to perform big responsibilities or tasks. Blonde, blue eyed, "cutsie-ness" is sometimes valued superficially, but often not internally or from a leadership development perspective. I am not always seen first for my intelligence, or my ability to speak well, or my ideas I contribute. Unfortunately, many women all over the world, and for many years, have experienced this sort of gender bias. People from all marginalized backgrounds experience similar barriers. It is important to remember that as leaders, we do not all have the same access to opportunities. I hope that someday I can bring more awareness to this issue and lead from a place of greater understanding of inequality in our work places.

■ **What processes and measures alert you to urgency in your system that we need to tend to? What are the early warning signs?**

I try to handle all the tasks I do as urgent and important. I prioritize my work by when it is due and how long it will take me to complete it. If I have something due Wednesday at 6:30 p.m. and something else due Friday at 6:00 p.m., but the Friday task is more important, I will still do Wednesday's work first and move forward to the Friday task. When stress begins to take over, the warning signs are the "glazed over" look in my eyes, and I tend to become more reclusive. I don't like stress, stress doesn't like me; I will lose sleep, have stress dreams, and even sometimes become physically ill. When someone catches me in those early stages and can see the warning signs, I can snap out of it quickly with some TLC from friends and people I'm close to. Sometimes I just need to put everything down and go to dinner with a friend and I'll feel better.

## Kelly's Responses

## What do I think/believe?

■ **Are you able to balance academic, professional and personal commitments? How does your current leadership style impact your ability to meet your overall life goals?**

I am a full-time student at school and have another part-time job on campus. During the summer, I work two jobs as a full-time intern and a part-time intern. I found balance between them by making a nice, organized schedule for myself to clearly show what to do at what time. I need to learn to practice my strengths more. I have them but I do not always exhibit them out of fear of judgment. As someone not originally from the United States, sometime I feel more comfortable in a learning mode. I just feel that I have so much to learn about the culture and the customs. However, by holding back my strengths and my leadership behaviors, I am not allowing my colleagues to see what I am truly capable of. I want to practice these skills and build on my strengths and leader capacities now so that I can grow into a strong professional leader as my career develops.

## What do I do?

■ **How do you take advantage of opportunities?**

There is an old saying that opportunities are left only to prepared minds. For that reason, I remind myself all the time that I need to prepare well to get opportunities. Once they come, besides simply finishing the tasks from the opportunities, taking advantage of them is one great way to upgrade myself. Therefore, every time I get a chance, I first think about what this opportunity can bring me, such as a new skill, or heavy use of a current skill. After analyzing what I will need to use in that opportunity, I will use that opportunity to improve whatever skill I use. Taking opportunities as challenges is a useful tool to discover my strengths and weaknesses, and

I can put my strengths into action. Most importantly, I need to capitalize on my strategic and communication skills to begin asking for opportunities from those who supervise or mentor me.

**How do you compensate for your weakness?**

One way I compensate for my weakness is to put more effort on what I am able to do rather than what I am not able to; instead of avoiding my weakness in front of people, I use my strengths to overcome it. For example, I know that I am not good at talking business via phone. This may be surprising considering my strength of communication, but I believe that I excel mostly in written communication. I sometimes can't organize the words that I have prepared in my mind, and I think that I sound awkward to people listening on the phone. However, my job requires me to make phone calls. Before I call, instead of preparing the words only in my mind—and that I might easily forget—I write them down on paper. I found that way works for me and gives me more confidence speaking aloud in the office. Facing a weakness is always how I encourage myself to overcome it. Of course, I sometimes ask others for help. I listen and learn from their experiences.

## What do we believe?

**Notice the various people and groups in your life (family, colleagues, boss, community, friends, etc.), what do they consider "urgent"?**

Different people have different definitions of urgency. My family would always consider health their top priority, so health problems are most urgent for my family. When I get sick, they always stop everything and come to take care of me. To them, there is nothing more important than a family's health. I will do the same thing for my parents. If they get seriously ill, I'll stop all the work and study, and go back to them. Right now, there is no need to worry about my family since they are all in good health. What is urgent now for me is to find a good job. As a senior in college, this is my top priority. And, the definition of urgent varies according to different levels of my life. For colleagues, finishing the work at hand and passing it to them is urgent. For bosses, making a clear business position and business strategy is urgent. For a community, establishing a complete system for everyone is urgent. "Urgency" varies depending on role or context. My strategic and individualization strengths allow me to decide how to categorize urgency with projects and people well.

**Determine how your sense of urgency connects with the group's sense of urgency based on its priorities, goals, and pain points.**

One essential ability to have in group work is understanding. I understand what needs to be achieved, what we need to do, and how we do it. This is definitely my strategic strength in action combined with my EIL capacity of empathy. By understanding my job, I am more confident to work through the steps to achieve our final, collective goal. Only when I fully understand the situation and status of work, and the perspective of the people involved, can I make accurate decisions on what is less important, or what is the priority and urgent. Knowing which role I play at work is also important. It helps me to know my position in teamwork so that I won't be doing things that are not necessary for me to do and, consequently, waste time. For example, if I am an intern, my job is to understand basic jobs; if I am a manager, my "urgency" may be to prepare proposal and presentations to the boss; if I am a boss, my urgency may be to meet with clients and maintain relationships with bosses from other companies. As a whole, understanding the nature of my work and my position is essential to connecting my sense of urgency with the groups.

## How do we do this?

■ **What groups or programs are enables or barriers that will impact my development?**

My classes, student organizations, and internship have been very supportive in my self-development. The knowledge I learn from lectures gives me a broad preview of the real world, the events I hold with schoolmates expands my network, and the actual work I do in internships improve my professional skills. Besides the professional side, every little moment in life could be a lecture for me—I learn things that are not taught in textbooks. They all enable me in the quest to improve myself.

I can think of a few barriers. The greatest one is cultural conflict. I am an international student studying English as a second language. My linguistic abilities and values differ from native citizens. My identity as an international student is one huge barrier that blocks me from many chances and jobs. The only way to survive is to put in more effort than local students who compete for the same thing. My strength of positivity allows me to be optimistic about my chances for job and allows me to persevere through the setbacks. The second barrier is that what I am truly interested in and what I am actually doing at work are different. I would like to be a marketing professional or buyer in fashion retail, yet none of my internships are about fashion. However, it is important to build basic marketing skills in different companies for my own development. But fashion retail is so specialized that you need to know the fashion market well, which is a totally different industry than industries like insurance. I have to have a fashion sense in order to be a successful fashion professional. My lack of experience in my dream area is a huge barrier. Nonetheless, I continue to work to overcome these barriers by using my creativity. If I can learn to capitalize on my strength of communication more, and overcome my fears of communicating with English as my second language, then I can likely network more effectively within the fashion industry.

## Evaluating Your Situation and Strengths

Now that you have followed the student responses, it's time to complete the worksheets. Based on your assessment results, if you have not done so already, complete the SWOT analysis in Table 3.1 and answer one to three questions from each section in Table 3.2 for yourself. By internalizing your strengths and opportunities, you can identify the gaps that, when filled, will help you to accomplish your vision. Understanding your weaknesses will also help you know what to avoid, what to improve, and what personal feedback to request from people skilled in those areas. Again, as a rule of thumb, focus about eighty percent of your development activities on areas that inspire you, and about twenty percent on areas you must address in order to move forward.

We encourage you to complete all of the exercises, taking your time and giving proper attention to gathering input from several different sources. When you have a clear picture of your strengths and opportunities, you will be ready to move to the next step. You may now find that you have a different or clearer perception about where you excel, and how those areas can complement your vision.

This chapter helped you clarify your strengths and opportunities for growth as a foundation for your personal transformation journey. Bear in mind that you are creating your own story through this process. The next chapter focuses on the framework for creating a development plan that will allow you to close the gap between your vision and where you are today.

**What do I think/believe?**

## What do I do?

## What do we believe?

## How do we do this?

# CHAPTER 4
## Step 3: Plan Your Journey

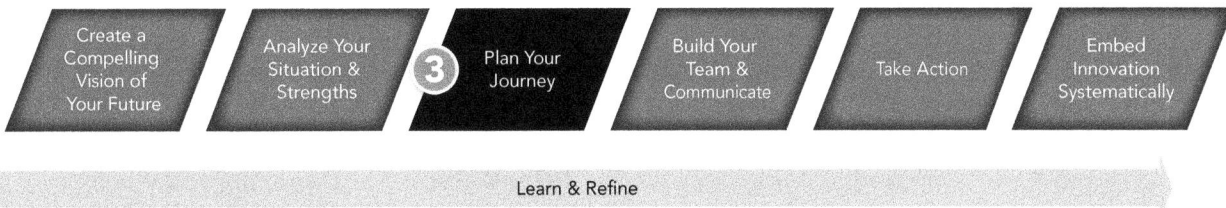

| Create a Compelling Vision of Your Future | Analyze Your Situation & Strengths | ③ Plan Your Journey | Build Your Team & Communicate | Take Action | Embed Innovation Systematically |

Learn & Refine

Once you have a solid plan for your development journey, you can begin investing your time and energy on your vision, your strengths and opportunities, and your development goals. In order to stay motivated, it is important to experience a sense of measurable growth. Tangible results are especially important to implementing change, and demonstrating progress is, naturally, part of the expectation. An example is: If my professor wants to see that I am a good student before she will give me a good grade, I need to show that I am "good" as measured by the professor's criteria. So, in this case, I would want to understand the criteria, as well as know what the professor values, and build a plan that allows me to show those results. On the other hand, if I am developing for my own personal growth, I may not be as concerned about showing results to others, but the self-evaluation process is just as important and I will still need to feel as if I am making progress. In fact, one important aspect of developing as a leader is learning to self-motivate simply for the goal of improvement, as opposed to improving to gain any sort of external reward.

In a senior-level leadership course I teach, I have students complete an assignment called "Giving Yourself an A." I borrowed this assignment from Benjamin Zander, conductor of the Philadelphia Philharmonic and author of *The Art of Possibility*. In the book, there is a chapter called "Giving an A" in which he outlines his observations of his students in his music performance class and their tendency to focus only on the small mistakes they made while playing rather than developing their broader ability as a musician and really leaning in to their potential. His idea was to take away the pressure of the grade and have students set their own standards for their growth and development in the course. So, he asked his students to write him a letter at the beginning of the semester outlining how they planned to earn their "A" in the course. Then, that paper became the rubric, or the measure of their success. Once they weren't concerned with how to live up to some "standard" set by the instructor, and instead began to consider what their unique developmental needs were as musicians, they were able to let go of the mistakes and focus on the growth.

I have adapted this for my leadership course and ask students to consider what they want to gain after reading through the syllabus and the requirements that I present. There are still required readings and assignments (all papers), but they can choose to emphasize or focus on a particular part of the course if they feel that is where they need to develop most. We meet to discuss their progress halfway through the course and at the end of the semester. The "Giving Yourself an A" assignment has transformed my classroom, increased engagement, and created positive learning moments for the students. I encourage you to consider how giving yourself an A before you begin a developmental journey can change the way you view the journey. As Zander wrote, "The practice of *giving* an A transports you and your relationships from the world of measurement into the world of possibility."

As you can imagine, some results will take longer than others to manifest. Our experience with student leaders has shown that they can certainly make quick progress in some areas, but headway in other areas may take years. Your life situation also impacts your development. For example, a student leader may be a great academic student, and this is a core value she holds. She might create meaningful results that help cultivate developmental growth by focusing on specific behaviors that will promote her well-being and academic success. In other words, she may simply experience a sense of progress ranging from a greater feeling of calm, clearer thinking, and better relationships with other students and that will lead to better performance. She may also see measured results quantitatively using an academic assessment of grades and getting feedback from friends showing significant improvements in key leadership-related qualities. Another student leader who wants to have a greater impact on the world may have an entirely different development focus and plan.

Consider the value of investing your energy in this journey as a way to foster meaningful change for the people closest to you. If you know, for example, that you have specific behaviors that are particularly difficult for your professor, an important team member, or a loved one, you may want to prioritize those areas for improvement.

## Development Plan Focus

As you begin building your capacity, you may want to consider two distinct, yet essential, areas: external capacity and internal capacity. Though the research emphasizing the importance of both is compelling, most of our formal training still focuses on hard skills (external capabilities). This exclusive emphasis leaves many leaders ill-prepared for, and in some cases uninformed about, the importance of internal capacity, such as emotional intelligence and interpersonal skills. When students look at leaders, they often don't realize the amount of effort these leaders have spent developing personal and internal characteristics and aspects to become strong leaders. This development is a major contributor to their success, and for many of the most successful leaders this is a lifelong focus on an "inside out" development practice. According to the MIT Slone Management Review March 2012 article, "How to become a better leader":

> "A survey of 75 members of the Stanford Graduate School of Business Advisory Council rated *self-awareness as the most important capability* for leaders to develop. Executives need to know where their natural inclinations lie in order to boost them or compensate for them. Self-awareness is about identifying personal idiosyncrasies—the characteristics that executives take to be the norm but actually represent the exception."

This is confirmed by the *Inc.* article based on the Change Style Indicator® with over 41,000 managers, "Although it is probably one of the least discussed leadership competencies, self-awareness is possibly one of the most valuable. Self-awareness is being conscious of what you're good at while acknowledging what you still have yet to learn. This includes admitting when you don't have an answer and culpability when you make a mistake. The article goes on to suggest that awareness of your strengths and weaknesses promotes an environment of trust.

> *"Internal capacity is largely underestimated by academia. Research done at the Carnegie Foundation for the Advancement of Teaching found that internal capacity, such as interpersonal skills, even in highly technical industries such as engineering, make up for about 85% of one's financial success, while 15% is due to technical knowledge."*
>
> —Dale Carnegie, *How to Win Friends and Influence People*

To take this a step further, we believe that as a leader you need to understand and live your values to be truly successful.

While this workbook is written for college students, it is important to begin building internal and external capacity throughout your leadership journey—starting at the very beginning. These terms are defined as:

- **External capacity (hard skills)** – Skills and behaviors associated with professional success. This is where many college classes and professional development efforts have been focused.

- **Internal capacity** – Includes intention, world view, purpose, vision, values, cultural norms, emotional stability, resilience, a sense of being grounded, overall personal well-being, intuition, balanced perspective, and attitude, and serves as the foundation for you to accomplish your deepest aspirations. Internal capacity is also required to move on to later stages of development.

In most organizations, the vast majority of development efforts focus on hard skills (including advanced degrees and certification programs) and, thus, many leaders need to balance them by explicitly exercising internal capacity. To further describe this process, we use the term *mastery*, which simply means the capacity to not only produce results, but also to master the principles underlying those results. In other words, as a master, you can deliver results comfortably due to the internal capacity behind your skills and judgment. Mastery of skills also contributes to leadership self-efficacy, or the belief in one's ability to engage in the action of leadership and the belief in one's capacity to learn the skills necessary to function as a leader. As mastery is developed, leaders must view failure as part of the process and practice self-correction, be open to learning new perspectives and skills, and develop resilient self-efficacy in moments of adversity.

Personal mastery involves enhancing your internal capacity to support the skills you have acquired while also removing barriers to your success. To help you achieve personal mastery, we recommend you enrich your ongoing development plan and personal practices (activities we repeat until we master them, like playing the piano or our golf swing).

To accomplish your vision, you may benefit from one or all of the following three developmental focuses:

- **Becoming more effective; developing new skills and/or behaviors** – In this category, the focus is on skills that can be developed through classes primarily, but also through extra-curricular activities such as sports, student organizations, and community involvement that will significantly impact performance. As you advance in your education and move into your career you will continually need to build new skills. These can range from an understanding of how to leverage social media to promoting your organization to public speaking. These can be external skills or internal skills, and the success of your efforts in changing behaviors and building skills will be measured by observable behavioral change.

- **Building on your current strengths** – Development can take the form of focusing on enhancing current strengths. It can also focus on important behaviors that adversely impact success. We recommend focusing eighty percent of your effort toward building your passions and the other twenty percent toward shoring up your deficiencies. This is a general recommendation. It is important to remember that your specific situation and needs will be clear indicators of what changes are required for your continued growth and success.

- **Minimizing your weaknesses** – In the SWOT analysis, you may have identified some behaviors that impede further growth. These may have been behaviors that made you successful in your current development (sometimes referred to as *overused strengths*). Even so, part of your development is examining the events and behaviors that got you here, and understanding which interfere with your success as defined by your vision. For example, you may identify yourself as someone who is on top of every task. As your responsibilities grow, you will delegate more, but you may still feel uncomfortable about your lack of knowledge of the details. Trying to manage the details to the degree that made you successful will become a weakness as you move up. It is important to tend to these behavioral changes as part of your plan. The challenge here may be shifting the focus away from daily details toward strategic thinking and expanding your ability beyond one or a few core strengths to develop several additional capabilities.

There are some important factors to consider when creating your plan. First, just as in physical training, you will get more leverage if you cross-train or develop several areas at the same time. According to Ken Wilber, a leading philosopher, there are benefits to cross-training beyond simply focusing on one area. For example, people who both lift weights and meditate tend to make greater improvements in both areas than those who only do one or the other. Evidence suggests that a combination of activities from different parts of our lives complement one another. This is quite true in the leadership arena as well.

A comprehensive plan will take into consideration each of the dimensions that are foundational to the human experience: physical, emotional, mental, and spiritual (people not comfortable with the term *spiritual* can substitute *altruistic* or *purpose*). If any of these elements are neglected, you are likely to find that it will adversely impact your success in other areas over the long term.

> *"I underestimated how spiritual/altruistic/purpose dimensions impact my goals, and my life has changed since considering them. I find my goals less superficial and more fulfilling. By looking for unique ways to impact the world, I began to see that leadership is as much about affecting change as it is about being at the top of a hierarchy. This was an empowering exercise that changed my life."*

—Eric Philippou

There are standard programs designed to help this process. One of the programs we suggest is Integral Transformative Practice (ITP), developed by Michael Murphy and George Leonard. This practice involves a strong cross-training routine. Nine commitments form the essential building blocks of the ITP program. They create the roadmap for practitioners to follow to realize their potential through the cross-training of body, mind, heart, and soul. The commitments include aerobic exercise, mindful eating, strength training, staying emotionally current, a service component, and the ITP Kata, which is a 40-minute series involving movements derived from yoga and Aikido, deep relaxation techniques, imagery, affirmations, and meditation. ITP is a long-term program for realizing the potential of body (exercise), mind (reading, discussion), heart (staying emotionally current, community), and soul (meditation, affirmations). Joining a local ITP group can augment a strong individual practice. ITP is available on DVD if you want to practice it solo, or in groups with friends. You may want to seek out similar programs on campus. Many campuses offer yoga and mindfulness classes through recreation or wellness centers. If you are a distance learner, you may want to find similar programs in your community

## Tools and Exercises

The range of tools is quite broad, so it is important to select something that feels safe and consistent with your values. The objective is to create a plan that you can follow and stick with to accomplish your goals. To help you get started, we put suggestions in Table 4.1. While several items fall within multiple categories, we attempted to classify them to be as mutually exclusive as possible. Some activities will provide benefits across several categories. An example is meditation or mindfulness practice, as it can help you manage your negative thinking, improve focus, balance emotions, and improve decision-making capacity. Even professional sports teams are beginning to realize the importance of focusing the mind as a part of success. The Seattle Seahawks' coaching staff has added meditation and yoga to the everyday practice routine to help build resiliency in the face of stress, optimism, and happiness among the players. More than twenty players commit weekly to these optional sessions with the team's sport psychologist (Roenigk, 2013).

Healthy development encompasses work in all areas. The practices you choose may evolve, and your practice may fluctuate based on other life demands. We encourage you to maintain as much consistency as possible. Just as the benefit of exercise increases when you hit a specific frequency and duration, the same will be true for leadership development practices. The more you invest, the better your results will be.

## TABLE 4.1: RECOMMENDATIONS FOR INTERNAL AND EXTERNAL CAPACITY BUILDING - ACTIVITIES TO CONSIDER INCORPORATING INTO PLAN

**What activities can I do to impact my internal capacity (what I think and believe)?**

- **Spirit**
  - Define vision
  - Define values
  - Pray
  - Participate in religious practices
  - Religious study
  - Seek spiritual counseling
  - Seek a spiritual teacher
  - Visualize goals
  - Become socially active – volunteer
- **Ethics**
  - Create guiding principles or values
  - Pay attention to ethics around you
  - Address situations you find unethical
  - Read and learn about ethics
- **Emotions (Emotional Quotient)**
  - Meditate
  - Seek therapy
  - Practice HeartMath techniques
  - Practice shadow exercises – the ability to find in yourself the things you find frustrating in others and address them as growth opportunities
  - Keep a journal
  - Seek coaching
  - Maintain strong friendships

**What activities can I do to impact my external capacity?**

- **Body**
  - Exercise
  - Yoga
  - Relaxation
  - Weight lifting
  - Mindful eating/healthy diet
  - Sufficient sleep
- **Mind**
  - Read
  - Study
  - Attend lectures and discussion groups
  - Attend school
  - Perspective-taking exercises (see online resources)
  - Take stretch assignments
  - Volunteer for opportunities to build skills (volunteer work)
  - Manage polarities (see book resources)
  - Action inquiry (see book resources)
  - Mindfulness-Based Stress reduction (see CD resources – Mindfulness in action)
- **Cross Training**
  - Integral Transformative Practice (yoga, aikido, relaxation, visualization, meditation)
  - Reflection practices (do-reflect-learn)

**What activities can I do that impact us as a group (what we think/believe)?**

- Review the list above, and determine which activities can be completed in a group. What groups do I participate in, and do they have similar values?
- Develop a mission and values as a family, or the group that serves as your family now. You may choose to set meditation time or gym time to promote a commonsense of focus and well-being. Many families share religious traditions and find that they provide a solid foundation and a shared set of values

**What structures and/or groups will help? What groups or programs do I participate in?**

- Activities could include how we eat, our exercise routines, our church or spiritual practice, and our volunteer activities
- Friend/social activities include what I do with my friends that support and that hinder my development, such as exercise groups, emotional support, honest and accurate feedback, and dialogue practices
- Work events and support, including yoga classes, weight management support, fitness classes, insurance discounts for fitness, and smoking cessation programs
- Practice groups for development, such as Integral Transformative Practice, meditation, and church
- Study groups
- Formal education programs
- Informal education programs
- Fitness groups and programs, such as running clubs, ski clubs, exercise groups, and gym memberships

The following is a development plan template designed to help you create a plan that allows you to achieve your goals. This table focuses mainly on identifying opportunities and the intentions behind your desire to change. This table is used to refine your areas of developmental focus. It will help you determine which areas from your SWOT analysis should be included in your development plan. You may find as you work through these questions that it serves as a filter for how you choose to focus your energy.

## TABLE 4.2: EVALUATE AND SELECT SKILL/BEHAVIORAL CHANGE PRIORITIES

| Key Actions | Detailed Action Planning | Behavior 1 |
|---|---|---|
| Select behaviors | Which behaviors do I want to improve or change?<br><br>Which behaviors do I perform well that I would like to enhance? | |
| What are the consequences of this behavior? | What will happen if I continue to demonstrate this behavior in the future?<br><br>How will my behavior impact service recipients?<br><br>How will it impact my career?<br><br>How will it impact my colleagues?<br><br>How will my behavior impact the organization? | |
| Why do I demonstrate this behavior? | I have developed behaviors over the course of my life because they made sense.<br><br>What has changed to make this behavior ineffective now? | |
| How would I like to perform in the future? | Write an end-result statement describing the changes I will make and the impact of those changes. What will an observer see when I have made these changes? | |
| Who will help me change? In the next section you will identify specific people who can help. | Who could I ask to provide me with feedback on how I am doing?<br><br>Who could be a good mentor? | |
| What type of support do I want? | Make an agreement with a person I trust about how I would like us to support one another in changing behaviors.<br><br>How will that person hold me accountable for taking this step?<br><br>How will I support him in changing his behavior?<br><br>Is there a group that will support me in the long term? | |

| Key Actions | Detailed Action Planning | Behavior 1 |
|---|---|---|
| What will I do or not do? | What other actions could I take? What am I willing to commit to doing? What am I committed to stopping? | |
| When will I complete actions? | When will I have completed action items? | |

## EVALUATE AND SELECT SKILL/BEHAVIORAL CHANGE PRIORITIES - ANTHONY

| Key Actions | Detailed Action Planning | Behavior 1 |
|---|---|---|
| Select behaviors | Which behaviors do I want to improve or change? Which behaviors do I perform well that I would like to enhance? | A behavior that I would like to improve is to become more focused on active listening when I first meet someone. This would include paying attention to people's names, understanding what they do for a living, or what is important to them. I believe these qualities are essential for building good business and personal relationships. <br><br> Enhance: Balancing time management based on priorities, establishing realistic timelines, and returning messages, such as e-mail in a timelier manner. |
| What are the consequences of this behavior? | What will happen if I continue to demonstrate this behavior in the future? How will my behavior impact service recipients? How will it impact my career? How will it impact my colleagues? How will my behavior impact the organization? | If I continue with poor active-listening skills, it will be more difficult to establish successful business and personal relationships. My career would be negatively impacted because important information will not be internalized to fulfill my job responsibilities. In addition, my colleagues will not be able to trust that I will complete or participate in assignments fully since I may not understand the entirety of the job. My organization will potentially lose customers since my attention to important details regarding customers is incomplete. <br><br> Enhance: I will develop strategies to enhance my ability to retain information about customers, use timelines with my colleagues to complete projects, and develop a stable base of consumers for my organization. |
| Why do I demonstrate this behavior? | I have developed behaviors over the course of my life because they made sense. What has changed to make this behavior ineffective now? | These behaviors have developed because my circle of contacts was relatively small until college. A small circle of friends allowed for the repetition of information over a long period of time. This extended time period allowed me to slowly integrate and remember key facts. As my circle of contacts rapidly increases, it will be important to integrate information through active listening at a much faster pace. In addition, the information is more complex and in-depth. |

| Key Actions | Detailed Action Planning | Behavior |
|---|---|---|
| How would I like to perform in the future? | Write an end-result statement describing the changes I will make and the impact of those changes. What will an observer see when I have made these changes? | I will make a greater effort to actively listen to those I meet in business and on a personal level. This change will help enhance my relationships through utilizing information to better serve my customers. Being a better and more active listener will mean that I will actually be more interested in someone and what he is saying because I'm fully engaged in the moment. Observers will note that my interactions are more genuine because I am committed to those moments. |
| Who will help me change? In the next section you will identify specific people who can help. | Who could I ask to provide me with feedback on how I am doing? Who could be a good mentor? | Key at this stage of my life are professors who give me feedback on how I am improving. I can learn from a good mentor in my family, and experienced business colleagues. |
| What type of support do I want? | Make an agreement with a person I trust about how I would like us to support one another in changing behaviors. How will that person hold me accountable for taking this step? How will I support him in changing his behavior? Is there a group that will support me in the long term? | I will help support behaviors that are beneficial to our mutual success. Complete honesty and firm reminders will help keep us accountable to each other's change. I will try to model good behaviors and point out poor behaviors when I experience or see them. My close colleagues in business and family members will hold be accountable for achieving these goals of improved active listening. |
| What will I do or not do? | What other actions could I take? What am I willing to commit to doing? What am I committed to stopping? | I will keep a running written daily calendar of events and people that I have met and the important information I have heard from them. I will seek feedback and repeat the information I hear from my customers and friends to make sure I fully understand what they have said or are asking. I am committed to ending poor listening skills and being more actively engaged in what others have to say. |
| When will I complete actions? | When will I have completed action items? | This will be a lifelong goal, but I would like to see improvements within four months since I will be graduating in December. I will be able to incorporate the self-evaluation information in my new job setting to increase my potential of being successful. |

## EVALUATE AND SELECT SKILL/BEHAVIORAL CHANGE PRIORITIES – SHELBY

| Key Actions | Detailed Action Planning | Behavior 1 |
|---|---|---|
| Select behaviors | Which behaviors do I want to improve or change? Which behaviors do I perform well that I would like to enhance? | One behavior I would like to work on is talking too much or talking over people when they are speaking. I am aware that I do this and sometimes annoy myself when having conversations with people. I sometimes am so excited about relating to others that I start sharing my thoughts before they are finished. It is horribly rude and I want to be better at listening fully before taking my turn.<br><br>I am really great with body language and non-verbal when I'm communicating with others. I tend to be hyper-aware of how I stand or sit, what my face looks like, and what my hands are doing when I am talking to people. |
| What are the consequences of this behavior? | What will happen if I continue to demonstrate this behavior in the future? How will my behavior impact those around me? How will it impact my career? How will it impact my colleagues? How will my behavior impact the organization? | I'm afraid that if I don't change this behavior, people will start thinking I'm rude, disrespectful, or that I don't care what they are saying or talking about. In the workplace, it is vital to be a good listener, as well as a good communicator. Listening is a part of communicating, and I need to be well rounded in communication skills to be respected and liked in my chosen career. My colleagues will want to know I am listening. My leaders will want me to listen. My behavior will have a direct impact on how I am viewed and treated at work. |
| Why do I demonstrate this behavior? | I have developed behaviors over the course of my life because they made sense. What has changed to make this behavior ineffective now? | I was painfully quiet and shy until the age of 16 or 17. I think as I became more confident in myself and my abilities, I became more excited to talk and get to know people. What has changed is that I know this behavior of interrupting or talking too much is a detriment to both my personal and professional development. Others need to know that I'm listening to, or have heard, them. |
| How would I like to perform in the future? | Write an end-result statement describing the changes I will make and the impact of those changes. What will an observer see when I have made these changes? | I will use my strengths in nonverbal and verbal communication to make a change in how I listen and have conversations with others. An observer will note that I nod my head to show understanding, rather than interrupting with a verbal assent; my face will show a focus on the speaker, rather than an anxiousness to speak that shows on my face. |
| Who will help me change? | Who could I ask to provide me with feedback on how I am doing? Who could be a good mentor? | I will need to rely on my friends who aren't afraid to critique me and my behaviors. I have a few very close friends who keep it real with me and will say how I'm doing. |

| Key Actions | Detailed Action Planning | Behavior 1 |
|---|---|---|
| What type of support do I want? | Make an agreement with a person I trust about how I would like us to support one another in changing behaviors. How will that person hold me accountable for taking this step? How will I support him in changing his behavior? Is there a group that will support me in the long term? | I plan on making an agreement with a coworker/best friend. He sees me in a professional and a personal environment daily so he has the unique ability to critique my behaviors at work and at play. I need to be sure I am open and welcoming to his feedback and observations and that I don't get upset or defensive. |
| What will I do or not do? | What other actions could I take? What am I willing to commit to doing? What am I committed to stopping? | Because I believe I am self-aware, I need to take that knowledge and apply it to all of my behaviors. I am committed to checking myself when I'm having conversations and to taking turns when speaking with others. |
| When will I complete actions? | When will I have completed action items? | I will complete these action items before the start of the new year! |

## EVALUATE AND SELECT SKILL/BEHAVIORAL CHANGE PRIORITIES – KELLY

| Key Actions | Detailed Action Planning | Behavior 1 |
|---|---|---|
| Select behaviors | Which behaviors do I want to improve or change? Which behaviors do I perform well that I would like to enhance? | Improve: Be brave, speak out about my ideas/opinions while working in a group. Not be afraid to network and meet new people.<br><br>Enhance: Creativity. I would like to start using my creativity in more fashion-related ways and in everyday life. |
| What are the consequences of this behavior? | What will happen if I continue to demonstrate this behavior in the future? How will my behavior impact service recipients? How will it impact my career? How will it impact my colleagues? How will my behavior impact the organization? | Improve: If I can be brave and speak out more, I can help contribute more ideas, showing my abilities and value, and make career connections, rather than just listening and working quietly with the team.<br><br>Enhance: Being creative in life and fashion will help me reach my career goals. It will also help me be interesting to—and valued by—my colleagues, which will help the success of my career and eventually my company. |
| Why do I demonstrate this behavior? | I have developed behaviors over the course of my life because they made sense. What has changed to make this behavior ineffective now? | Improve: When I was young my behavior was very different. I always hid behind people. In my culture people tend to be less assertive than in the US. Additionally, my personality is introverted and shy.<br><br>Enhance: I have become less creative in fashion because I have worked at non-fashion internships. Also, I have become less creative in general because I have focused mainly on school, leaving little time for my creative interests. |
| How would I like to perform in the future? | Write an end-result statement describing the changes I will make and the impact of those changes. What will an observer see when I have made these changes? | Improve: I will eventually not just be a "team member," but an opinion and team leader. I will speak confidently in a wide range of settings, sharing my ideas and effectively expressing a different point of view. I will also be confident meeting new people and networking.<br><br>Enhance: I will try to apply my creativity in all aspects of my life, but primarily focus on fashion. Observers will see me constantly trying new things as I put my creative thoughts into actions. |
| Who will help me change? | Who could I ask to provide me with feedback on how I am doing? Who could be a good mentor? | Anyone who has experience and good personality traits can be strong examples for me. My colleagues, boss, friends, family, etc. I particularly look to strong women who model the traits that I want to develop. |

| Key Actions | Detailed Action Planning | Behavior 1 |
|---|---|---|
| What type of support do I want? | Make an agreement with a person I trust about how I would like us to support one another in changing behaviors. How will that person hold me accountable for taking this step? How will I support him in changing his behavior? Is there a group that will support me in the long term? | I need someone who can always encourage me and hear me. I know that I need to change, but I lack the courage. The person should be someone I trust, and should be more open and outgoing than I am. It would be helpful to have someone who is on a team with me to encourage me to participate more actively, introduce me to new people, and also help me feel safe.<br><br>I would like to have someone who already is a strong networker and has the ability to speak out professionally so I can learn things that I lack, and in return help him/her to improve. |
| What will I do or not do? | What other actions could I take? What am I willing to commit to doing? What am I committed to stopping? | This is a long way to go because first I need to break a psychological barrier, the fear of speaking in front of others and being rejected.<br><br>That requires me to encourage myself and build confidence day by day. I will do weekly reviews of my performance and track my progress. I can grow in this area by being less careful and using my creative and detail-oriented strengths more to make sure I am confident in what I saying. I will redirect my thoughts to apply and voice my creative thinking to the world around me. |
| When will I complete actions? | When will I have completed action items? | Breaking mental barriers is a long process, but my weekly reviews and talking to someone who can consistently support me will help to speed up the process. My goal is to improve my behavior in six months, but I may require more time. |

The next template was designed to synthesize development activities reflected in the prior worksheets.

We recommend that all goals be SMART, an acronym by George T. Doran referenced in the November 1981 issue of *Management Review*. SMART goals comprise five characteristics:

- **Specific** - Goals should be definitive and clearly defined. When goals are specific, it is clear to see when they are reached. To make goals specific, they must clarify exactly what is expected, why it is important, who's involved, where it is going to happen. *Overall example of a goal: Teachers want to improve the reading levels of all the children in their program by 25% in one school year to ensure their future academic success.*

- **Measurable** - Establish concrete criteria for measuring progress toward the attainment of each goal you set. Measurable defines what and how much change we are expecting. *Example: 25% in one school year is the measurement.*

- **Attainable** - When you identify goals that are most important to you, you begin to figure out ways you can make them come true. You develop the attitudes, abilities, skills, and financial capacity to reach them. You begin seeing previously overlooked opportunities to bring yourself closer to the achievement of your goals. "Attainable" ensures that our expectations are reasonable. *Example: One school year and 25% are reasonable goals; 80% in one semester is not an attainable goal.*

- **Realistic** - To be realistic, a goal must represent an objective toward which you are both *willing* and *able* to work. A goal can be both high and realistic. You are the only one who can decide the height of your goal, but be sure that every goal represents substantial progress. "Realistic" ensures we have the capacity to meet our goal. *Example: 25% is realistic—children can improve their reading levels that percentage in a year.*

- **Timely** - A goal should be grounded within an approximate time frame. Goals lacking time frames also lack urgency. Being timely ensures we have a deadline to meet our goals. As Dan Heath and Chip Heath state in *Switch: How to Change Things When Change is Hard*, "Some is not a number. Soon is not a time." *Example: One school year is a defined period of time.*

Using the information from the worksheets and templates provided, you are now ready to complete your Development Planning Worksheet. This worksheet will serve as the foundation for the actions you will take to accomplish your goals, and should reflect data you gathered in the assessment chapter and your personal reflection.

### TABLE 4.3: DEVELOPMENT PLANNING WORKSHEET

| Current State | Future State/Goal | Actions | By When? | Measure – How do you know? |
|---|---|---|---|---|
| | | | | |
| | | | | |
| | | | | |
| | | | | |
| | | | | |

## DEVELOPMENT PLANNING WORKSHEET – ANTHONY

| Current State | Future State/Goal | Actions | By When? | Measure – How do you know? |
|---|---|---|---|---|
| I have difficulty with active listening when I first meet someone and often cannot retain details from that first meeting. | I will be able to recall and retain important information that is discussed when I initially meet someone. | I will have a written daily calendar of events and people I have met and the important information I have heard from them.<br><br>I will have a weekly meeting with a trusted colleague and mentor for feedback on improved actively listening skill development. | I will see improvement in active listening skills within one week.<br><br>I will see significant and consistent retention of information within four months. | I will note how many times I do not retain personal information such as a name when interacting with individuals on a continuous basis.<br><br>I will review my ability to initiate conversation based on information retention from a previous meeting. |
| "Learner" is one of my top 5 strengths on the Strengths Finder assessment which means that I am continually seeking learning opportunities for personal growth. | About to be graduating from college does not mean being a student stops learning. Entering into the work force with no experience means a shift from being a student in the classroom to the office. Learn everything that I can to become an asset to any company I am with. | I will take notes and listen to the employees that I am going to be working with. Know that I don't know everything, so make sure to adsorb everything I can early on and continue with that approach all my life. | Being a student will never stop but I will make sure to take time out of my day at the end of each week and review key concepts, deadlines meet, people I have meet, etc. | I will make sure that I hold myself accountable and also make sure that at least once a month I can sit down with someone from the office and discuss future plans, deadlines, and continue to learn from them. |

### Anthony's Developmental Journey Continued

| Current State | Future State/Goal | Actions | By When? | Measure – How do you know? |
|---|---|---|---|---|
| I have a tendency to exhibit in unhealthy or unproductive behaviors. The one I was surprised about was learning how my strengths can also be a challenge when not used properly. My achiever strength can definitely motivate me, but if I am not as interested in a particular task, then I use my achiever strength in areas that are not my focus. I achieve in my social life, for example, instead of my schoolwork. I need to stay focused and motivated on the things that will propel me toward my future goals. | Motivation is crucial for being a college student and a college graduate. I had to have motivation to job search, motivation to complete schoolwork on time. Motivation is going to be different out in the work place. | Staying motivated at the end of semester with major projects to complete is difficult because you just want to be done. One way that I get through the lack of motivation is to take one task at a time, and make sure to stay enthusiastic about the work I am doing.<br><br>After graduation out in the workplace, I will have to continue to take it one step at a time and think, "How can I be the best asset to the company?"<br><br>I will also use my achiever strength and create checklists and a list of priorities for what needs to happen first, next, etc. I will use my learner strength to stay engaged and focus on the parts of the job that interest me and remain curious about all aspects of my work. | I will make sure to do a self-evaluation each week to make sure that I am doing everything I can for the company. | Meetings with bosses and self-evaluations will help me achieve and increase my motivation and be more enthusiastic about the work I am doing. |

## DEVELOPMENT PLANNING WORKSHEET – SHELBY

| Current State | Future State/ Goal | Actions | By When? | Measure – How do you know? |
|---|---|---|---|---|
| Sometimes, I just talk too much and am too loud. | I will let other people talk when it's their turn. I will self regulate how much I talk, as well as the volume of my voice. | I will leverage my strength in communication to become an even better communicator; talking when necessary at a level that is necessary for the situation. | I will work on this for the next four months with the help of my coworker/best friend. | Measuring this goal will be slightly difficult, but I think if I utilize my close friends and family to help me analyze my behavior(s), I will know if I am a becoming better with economy and volume of language. |
| I can be stubborn, not easily swayed when I make up my mind | I balance following through with my commitments with being open minded and curious. I listen to others' point of view with an open mind. | I build on my strengths as a communicator and I listen openly with an open heart and open mind. | I will work on this for the next four months with the help of my coworker/best friend. | I will measure this by paying attention to how often I "feel" like I have dug my heels in and need to defend my position from others. |

## DEVELOPMENT PLANNING WORKSHEET - KELLY

| Current State | Future State/ Goal | Actions | By When? | Measure – How do you know? |
|---|---|---|---|---|
| I have strong work experience and experience in student organization activities. I have many opportunities to speak up in a team, give ideas, and network. But I still have some fear inside and keep my thoughts and ideas to myself. | To be a stronger communicator within a team; be an opinion leader and good networker. | Daily encouragement before work; weekly review of performance; seek help from my mentor; be active and talk to new people at work. I will use my strategic strength to set goals. I can also use my strengths of woo to try to "win others over" through my creative ideas. | Six months or more | Check my performance reviews; maintain a log tracking number of times I spoke in meetings and projects; feedback from others and how they evaluate my ideas. Track my number of new connections. |
| I think creatively, but don't apply it to my life and in pursuit of my fashion career. | I actively apply my creativity and have some fashion experience either from work or other involvements. | Seek job opportunities in fashion even if they are only part-time. Find organization, or more friends to work on creative/ fashion projects with. Tap into my strength of positivity to build self-confidence around my creative abilities. By giving myself positive pep talks, perhaps I can share my ideas more openly with others. | Six months | By the number of creative/fashion related projects I am working on, even if they are small, and by my ability to see these situations as positive even when I am struggling. |

## Real World Application

### Time Management

For this real-world application exercise, make sure you have completed the Skills/Behavior Development Worksheet (4.2) and the Development Planning Worksheet (4.3). Now that you have identified some smaller goals (compared to life-time goals from previous chapters), we will use time management tools to fit these goals into your daily schedule with ease. Everyone will have a different method for what works for them. It will be important for you to select one that fits your style and strengths. We encourage you to be creative in how you approach goal-setting and to find your own unique way.

To illustrate one possible approach to goal setting, we will provide a structured example. Choose a digital calendar such as Google Calendar or the Calendar application for Mac—something with cloud capabilities so you can access it from multiple devices. Map out what your daily and weekly schedules look like. Create color-coded time blocks for events such as classes (specific name/ number) work, meetings, and then create time blocks for studying at the library and meal breaks; be sure to narrow down time blocks to the exact minute that they start and end. After you've done this, look for time in your schedule to include internal capacity exercises (stimulating the spirit, personal ethics, and emotions) and external capacity exercises (stimulating the body, mind, or the previous two at the same time). Perhaps do 30 minutes of internal and 30 minutes of external back-to-back, or vice-versa. And then, of course, map out time to focus on some of the goals you chose in your Development Planning Worksheet (4.3). Put the deadline in the digital calendar, maybe even consider downloading a countdown clock app for your computer or mobile device (there are many free countdown apps out there, choose any one of them). The most important thing you want to label on your daily/weekly schedule is *free time*. Refer to this calendar several times a day and when scheduling temporary events. If you're having trouble pushing yourself to start a particular scheduled task, or are simply forgetting to do it, set up notification alerts to remind you of the task.

### Innovative Leadership Reflection Questions

To help you develop your action plan, it is time to further clarify your direction using reflection questions. The questions for "What do I think/believe?" reflect your intentions. "What do I do?" questions reflect your actions. The questions "What do we believe?" reflect the culture of your organization (i.e., work, school, community), and "How do we do this?" questions reflect systems and processes for your organization. This exercise is an opportunity to practice innovative leadership by considering your vision for yourself and how it will play out in the context of your life. You will define your intentions, actions, culture, and systems in a systematic manner.

Table 4.4 contains an exhaustive list of questions to appeal to a broad range of readers. You will likely find that a few of these best fit your own personal situation. Focus on the questions that seem the most relevant. We recommend that you answer one to three questions from each of the categories.

## TABLE 4.4: QUESTIONS TO GUIDE THE LEADER AND ORGANIZATION

**What do I think/believe?**

- What are my priorities for development? Are they reflected in the plan I created?
- Am I willing to make the changes necessary to meet my goals?
- What do I consider personal short-term wins?
- Which wins do I want to see in what time frame? Is this reasonable?
- What do I consider a win for my group?
- Which short-term wins will be really important to key people in my life?
- How do I stay motivated to work toward goals that will take a long time or a lifetime to accomplish?
- Have I taken into account the whole range of activities I need to create a sustainable change, such as involving others and creating a plan that I can live with long term?

**What do I do?**

- How do I translate my vision into long- and short-term goals?
- Are my goals SMART? Why or why not?
- What are my financial goals and milestones?
- Is this a plan that is sustainable in the long term? Will accomplishing my short-term wins motivate me to stay on track with my long-term plan?
- Does my plan contain the foundation work as well as skill building (example: basic health as well as professional competencies)?
- Which wins can I identify and support that solve problems and are seeds for future shifts?
- Which changes in my behavior will demonstrate a strong statement to others and encourage their ongoing support, while possibly modeling changes that could also serve them?

**What do we believe?**

- Which wins will provide meaningful tangible and emotional results, and gain support of key stakeholders in my life?
- Which wins will encourage others to engage in their own personal/professional growth initiatives?
- Which stories can we tell others about the wins that were shared with the organization to encourage them to focus on their own development?
- Which wins are reinforced by our culture and values? Which wins would be opposed to our culture and values?

**How do we do this?**

- How do I align my goals and short-term wins with the university such that I receive support for the changes I am making? How do I ensure that early wins are important to key stakeholders (professors, coaches, bosses, friends, parents)?
- How do I track and measure my wins and their impact against overall personal and academic goals? Do I have early warning measures?
- Are my wins aligned with the larger objectives of my groups and communities?
- Do the groups that I am involved with reinforce and reward the behavioral changes I am making?

We will now walk through answers to one or two questions from each section of Table 4.4. Simply follow along with Anthony's, Shelby's and Kelly's responses to the questions for yourself, or select the questions that fit your current situation.

## Anthony's Reflection Responses

### What do I think/believe?

■ *Which short-term wins will be really important to key people in my life?*

Change is inevitable. Long-term change is a series of short-term changes that are beneficial to the end goal. A short-term win that focuses simply on remembering an individual's name when meeting, will test my active listening skills. Reviewing my informational log of my encounters will aid in my memory of specific details about an individual. In addition being able to balance my time and prioritize tasks, it will allow me to make time for the key people in my life. It will reduce my stress level when I have a large non-prioritized task list and make the time more meaningful with those I care about.

■ *What are my priorities for development? Are they reflected in the plan I created?*

My priorities for development are active listening, including increasing my ability to retain information about customers, businesses, and organizations that will aid in my success in business. My plan is to seek feedback from my written daily contact list, mentors, and colleagues regarding my abilities to retain information over time through active listening.

### What do I do?

■ *Are my goals SMART? Why or why not?*

My first specific goal is to retain more information through active listening when first introduced to individuals in business and personal life situations. It is a measurable goal since I can give a recap of the information I retain over time regarding my contacts. I believe it is attainable through developing active listening skills and reinforcing the information by direct feedback from the individual, and repetition of names and information in immediate conversations. A realistic goal is one that is achievable. This goal is achievable through several short-term strategies that include documenting conversation information and repeating information in a prompt manner. A timely goal is achievable in a specific time frame. I believe the four-month time frame for improvement in this skill is achievable. I also learned from taking the *StrengthsFinder* assessment that I need to learn to capitalize on my strengths to achieve my goals. So, how I approach SMART goals and how someone else might approach setting goals will look different—that was helpful as I set the goals listed below.

The second SMART goal that I can improve on is actually focusing on building my strength of learner in all arenas, especially in those areas where I want to grow. I want to be a better student. This is not just a student in the classroom; it is being a student in the workplace and life itself. Making sure that I am always listening to what people have to say, taking notes, and reflecting. I don't know everything, and when I graduate and go into my new job, I am going to be a student at the company where I am and need to make sure I stay motivated. I will self-evaluate each week and hold myself accountable.

The third SMART goal, is improving motivation to do my best work. Staying motivated is difficult when faced with multiple tasks, but one way that I make sure to keep improving is to use my Achiever strength where I have a tendency to make lists and then tick off tasks one at a time. This is a constant reminder and something to continue to improve on day in and day out.

■ *Is this a plan that is sustainable in the long term? Will accomplishing my short-term wins motivate me to stay on track with my long-term plan?*

This plan reflects a desired lifelong change in my ability to actively listen to people and gain information. Early short term wins, such as being able to retain a person's name, will motivate me to develop methods to learn more about a person and be able to use that information to develop deeper relationships with them.

## What do we believe?

■ *Which stories can we tell others about the wins that were shared with the organization to encourage them to focus on their own development?*

Success stories regarding advancing the organization's mission through developing deeper business relationships with potential customers will encourage others to try the techniques of active listening and of being engaged through curiosity and learning. I believe that stories focusing on new client recruitment through relationship development and strategy implementation will have a positive impact on my colleagues. Stories of the ability to recall important personal events learned about from your client, such as birthdays, advanced education efforts, new positions or promotions, children's colleges, and likes or dislikes regarding food and cuisine, make for deeper business relationships since you are demonstrating a genuine interest in others' lives both personally and professionally. And then, role modeling an interest in all aspects of the company for my colleagues will hopefully inspire them to do the same.

## How do we do this?

■ *Are my wins aligned with the larger organizational objectives of my groups or communities?*

The objective of my organization is to become the market leader in the product or service delivery. New contacts, lead generation, and relationship development are significant success factors for new business. Retaining current customers is equally important. My plan is to develop deeper relationships with potential and existing customers, which should translate into increased sales, awareness, or utilization of our services to meet their needs.

- **Do the groups that I am involved with reinforce and reward the behavioral changes I am making?**

A successful organization will recognize the efforts made by its employees toward meeting its mission. My changes should translate into increased revenue for the organization. An organization can reward success through increased opportunity to learn other aspects of the business, bonuses, immediate and public recognition of a job well done, or helping to advance a career.


## Shelby's Reflection Responses


## What do I think/believe?

- **Which short-term wins will be really important to key people in my life?**

I see a win as being able to change how I behave with people in conversations. For example, I'm sitting with a friend at Starbucks and we are talking about a new restaurant we both want to try. She is talking about how good the menu sounds, and I interrupt and jump in to comment on how I think the omelet looks amazing. I'm aware how my current behavior shifts a topic in conversation and often cuts off the people I'm speaking with. Changing this behavior will be important to key people in my life because allowing them to finish a thought or a sentence lets them know that I am listening to them and that I think what they are saying is meaningful.

- **What are my priorities for development? Are they reflected in the plan I created?**

I need to prioritize self-regulation and self-awareness more than anything. I have to be tuned into my actions and behaviors one-hundred percent of the time for this to work. I need to be aware of my voice level, my nonverbal, and how I respond to and comment on information I receive. I think if I practice prioritizing internally first, my external behaviors will change more quickly and more effectively.

- **How do you stay motivated to work toward goals that will take a long time or a lifetime to accomplish?**

This is a goal I have been thinking about for a long time, and I am already intrinsically motivated to attain it. To stay motivated to work toward a goal that will take a long time to accomplish, I remind myself to "keep my eyes on the prize" and continue to look forward to what's next without losing sight of what is in front of me in the moment. The balance can be difficult, but I realize that my current behavior is one that will be viewed negatively in graduate school and in the workplace. I've already seen some of its negative affects in social situations. My dreams and goals must be kept in focus, and I know that changing this behavior will go a long way toward achieving my long-term goals.

## What do I do?

■ *Are my goals SMART? Why or why not?*

I believe that this particular goal is quite specific. It is measurable by the reactions I have from people I know. It is attainable and realistic; however, it will require great self-restraint and discipline—basically re-teaching myself. With regard to being timely, I believe that this shift in behavior will demand a long-term, lifetime commitment.

■ *Is this a plan that is sustainable in the long term? Will accomplishing my short-term wins motivate me to stay on track with my long-term plan?*

No one likes a conversation "hog" or someone who has a voice that takes over a whole room instead of the space between two chairs. Once I change this behavior, it will eventually become more natural and a part of my day-to-day existence. Short-term wins will help me to stay positive and motivated to attain my goal.

■ *How do I translate my vision into long- and short-term goals?*

Long-term: I want a job that I love where I am able to communicate often and focus on relationships and educational leadership. I want to master my self regulatory abilities in order to then reach my long-term goal.

Short-term: I will attain my long-term goals through reflection on my current work, and have an introspective nature when I am working with others. I will put others first in the moment and remember to keep my *Communication* strength focused and regulated.

## What do we believe?

■ *Which wins will encourage others to engage in their own personal/professional growth initiatives?*

When I win at introspection into my behaviors and actions, others will naturally feed off how I act and respond. I can use my ability to serve as a good role model and encourage others by talking to them openly and transparently about my goals. I find it motivating to hear success— and even "not so successful" stories—and I am comfortable doing the same.

## How do we do this?

■ *Does the university reinforce and reward the behavioral changes I am making?*

Not necessarily as a whole; however, I could see how individuals within the university who motivate, challenge, and lead me would reinforce and reward my behavior changes. To me, that is more motivating! I want to be challenged and reinforced by individuals that I respect and look up to.

## Kelly's Reflection Responses

### What do I think/believe?

- ***How do you stay motivated to work toward goals that will take a long time or a lifetime to accomplish?***

I am a very easily motivated person. I could be motivated by other people, what they have done, inspiring events, and encouraging words. I think this is likely my Positivity strength in action and my general ability to remain optimistic. I know my weakness better than anyone else so I always keep in mind what I should and shouldn't do. I set standards and goals for myself to follow so that I won't lose direction.

I see motivation everywhere, and I am also motivated by healthy competition. My friends or classmates who perform better than I do in social events or in classrooms could be the example of what I want to be. For example, some of friends are very articulate in professional settings. This is an area of improvement for me. After knowing who around me has this talent, I will set him or her as my goal or example, but I will also not let the success of others intimidate me from being myself. I am a self-motivated person, so it is quite easy for me to look for goals and set up standards to motivate myself.

While I will always be learning and growing, I expect to build strong skills in the area of courageous communication. These skills will become part of who I am over time.

### What do I do?

- ***How do I translate my vision into long- and short-term goals?***

For my long-term goal, I want to be an opinion leader in the fashion industry; my coworkers and friends all respect me as the leading power and the brain of the team.

For the short-term, I want to change my behavior and characteristics to be less afraid and nervous so that I can speak out about my ideas in front of people. I believe this is a basic skill that will enable me to become the opinion leader in a professional setting. Also, I want to be involved with more fashion projects in which I can use my creativity.

### What do we believe?

- ***Which wins will encourage others to engage in their own personal/professional growth initiatives?***

My win of being able to lead a team and boost my reputation will provide others with a good example to learn from, just like the younger me many years ago learning from other successful people to improve myself. I hope to be a role model for other young women as they navigate their professional development. I will share my success with other students and later with colleagues. As we talk about our challenges and how we are overcoming them, I think we will all become more effective and this will also allow me to continue to build my network.

## How do we do this?

■ *Does the university reinforce and reward the behavioral changes I am making?*

The reward within the university will be a possible impact on my class participation scores and growth in my student organizations.

My main motivation is building a long-term skill that will support my career success. I will change my behavior because I see it as a way to improve my ability to be an innovative leader. I believe that I will be rewarded later in life for the excellent results I bring to the organization by having my behavior changed and ability improved.

## Creating Your Development Plan

Now that you have followed plans for Anthony, Kelly, and Shelby it is time to complete your worksheets. Based on your assessment results, if you have not done so already, complete the SWOT analysis in Table 4.1 and answer one to three questions from each section in Table 4.2 for yourself. By internalizing your strengths, as well as opportunities, you can identify the gaps that, when filled, will help you accomplish your vision. Additionally, understanding your weaknesses will help you know what to avoid, what to improve, and what personal feedback to request from people skilled in those areas.

This chapter provided you with the tools and templates to create your development plan, and will help to close the gap between where you are today compared with your vision. The plan will greatly enhance your efforts toward actualizing where you want to be, as well as making a positive impact on the world. Keep in mind that it is easy to create a plan that is too ambitious or complex. We encourage you to commit to small changes you can complete and then update your plan after you have accomplished your initial goals. The next chapter focuses on selecting the guiding team that will help you implement your plan.

The following is a development plan template designed to help you create a plan that allows you to achieve your goals. This table focuses mainly on identifying opportunities and the intentions behind your desire to change.

## TABLE 4.5: SKILL/BEHAVIOR DEVELOPMENT WORKSHEET
**Evaluate and Select Skill/Behavioral Change Priorities – Worksheet**

| Key Actions | Detailed Action Planning | Behavior 1 |
|---|---|---|
| Select behaviors | Which behaviors do I want to improve or change? Which behaviors do I perform well that I would like to enhance? | |
| What are the consequences of this behavior? | What will happen if I continue to demonstrate this behavior in the future? How will my service recipients be impacted? How will my career be impacted? How will my colleagues be impacted? How will my organization be impacted? | |
| Why do I demonstrate this behavior? | I have developed behaviors over the course of my life because they make sense. What has changed to make this behavior ineffective now? | |
| How would I like to perform in the future? | Write an end-result statement describing the changes I will make and the impact of those changes. What will an observer see when I have made these changes? | |
| Who will help me change? | Who could I ask to provide me with feedback on how I am doing? Who could be a good mentor? | |
| What type of support do I want? | Make an agreement with a person you trust about how you would like to support one another in changing behaviors. How will that person hold me accountable for taking this step? How will I support them in changing their behavior? Is there a group that will support me in the long term? | |
| What will I do or not do? | What other actions could I take? What am I willing to commit to doing? What am I committed to stopping? | |
| When will I complete actions? | When will I have completed action items? | |

## What do I think/believe?

**What do I do?**

## What do we believe?

**How do we do this?**

# CHAPTER 5

## Step 4: Build Your Team and Communicate

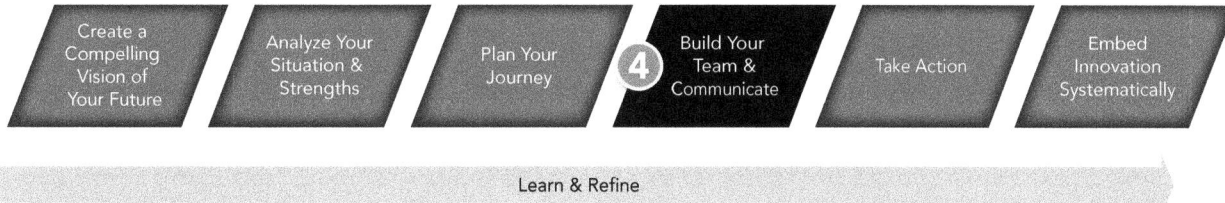

| Create a Compelling Vision of Your Future | Analyze Your Situation & Strengths | Plan Your Journey | ④ Build Your Team & Communicate | Take Action | Embed Innovation Systematically |

Learn & Refine

In this chapter, you will begin to identify the individuals you want to support your personal and professional development, and the specific roles you envision them playing during this transition. After selecting these people, you will consider the best ways to communicate your needs and receive their feedback. Here, you will carefully choose individuals you feel will be most supportive of your growth. Consider who is involved in your development and who is not. Your selection criteria should include: experience and skills in areas you want to develop, level of unconditional personal support, ability to offer constructive and valuable feedback, capacity to support your transformation, and ability to offer professional support and advocacy.

You will benefit from choosing a diverse yet trusted set of people to support your development. This is particularly beneficial if you plan to make changes that will significantly impact them as well. These people can come from various areas of your life, both family and school, and can have differing levels of involvement. Some, for example, could be fairly casual, such as a student who is willing to give you feedback after a class or team meeting about a specific behavior you may be experimenting with to meet a goal about improved interpersonal skills. At the other end of the continuum, you could engage in a more methodical, long-term agreement with a formal mentor or coach. You will also want to consider the role your partner plays if you are involved in a relationship. Anyone involved must agree to give you honest and supportive feedback. The common thread for the people you ultimately invite to share in your journey is a firm trust and belief that, above all else, their support is unquestionably in the interest and service of your growth and success.

As another option, your development support could be found within a team setting. For example, if your goal is to run a marathon, your development support could come from a range of sources. It could be as simple as joining a running group to support a fitness goal. You might recruit very specific individual running partners. Other options could include finding expertise from third-party sources like running magazines or online groups that discuss tips and progress. You may even select a group where the explicit purpose is to strongly hold each other more accountable.

*"When I seek mentors, I look for people who are top performers in their field, whether or not it's related to my field. True top performers, across all fields, have extremely strong internal capacity, and consciously work on it. I was a communication major in college. I had a mentor who won numerous Olympic medals and was a 10-time world champion in the sport of fencing; I learned more real-life skills from him than any of my professors."*

—Eric Philippou

Development can be supported in similar ways. You have a broad range of choices when looking for support. Organizations range from formal classes to formal and informal groups focused on specific skills or professional development opportunities. Many academic departments have student professional clubs related to future careers and some have formal mentoring programs already in place. Faculty can also serve as wonderful mentors. Student organizations offer informal mentoring opportunities from staff advisors and older peers. The key is to seek out involvement and opportunities to complement your personal goals. Depending on your needs, your individual selection of development support may have components of some or all of these choices. Some may be focused on hard skills, while others, like that of peer, staff, or faculty advisor/mentor, may take on a more generally supportive role. We also find that co-curricular activities provide great opportunities to build skills, such as emotional intelligence, and present the opportunity to learn to work well with others when you are leading and also when you are a team member.

After you have selected your support team, the next step will be deciding on methods for each person to communicate authentic feedback. This is the stage where you ask others for specific kinds of support, including possible behavioral changes on their part. You will be letting people around you know that you are engaged in a process of ambitious personal growth and that you want their feedback. Because people often create a sense of personal safety by being able to predict how others around them behave, it is important to inform the people closest to you that you are taking on a structured change process that may involve behaviors with which they are likely to be unfamiliar. The key message here should convey that this process will take time and you will use these new behaviors with varying levels of effectiveness until you master them. You may say you are changing and yet act inconsistently for some period of time while you master new skills.

While the information you share will change over time, the need for communication is critical throughout your development process. Communication will happen with different groups of people at various times, and will likely take on different tones depending on the audience and degree of impact. Some people will simply need to understand that overall change is underway. For example, a roommate or housemate may need to understand your goals if your sleep, study, or outside involvement changes dramatically in order to support you. The nature of your communication will depend on your relationship with the individual or group, and the type of support you are asking for.

During your process, you may also be asking others around you to change. For example, if you want to focus on becoming healthier, you may ask your friends to get together for yoga classes or sporting activities rather than lunch. As you model these new behaviors, be aware that some of your colleagues will adapt quite naturally, while others will require more specific and formal discussions to adjust to this new way of relating. As a team member on a class project, you may want to take on different tasks, as well as ask other teammates to participate in determining how they want to accomplish overall project tasks. In this case, you could open a dialogue exploring how assignments are made and how you will work together as a team to ensure all activities are accomplished effectively while everyone has the opportunity to learn new skills if they want. Though many students would respond favorably to the openness, some will likely be frustrated if you are not explicit with what you are trying to accomplish.

## *Support Team Selection Criteria*

Providing support to someone who is committed to a process of growth is an honor and a tremendous responsibility. It is important to select a support team judiciously since you are requesting these individuals to be trusted advisors.

The following is a rough list of key selection factors as a starting point for you to consider when selecting your team. You may find other factors that are also important to you.

**Performance:** Consider selecting people who have mastered concepts, skills, or behaviors that you would like to develop in yourself. Performance could be as simple as that person having expertise in your field, or in a field you want to explore. He or she could have strong interpersonal skills and empathy, or have hard skills such as financial analysis that you would like to enhance in yourself. These individuals could also be people you respect in general. If you are focused on developing advanced leadership skills, you could certainly benefit from the mentoring and support of someone you believe is successful against these measures.

**Family, friends and roommates:** People from your family supporting your development could include siblings, partners, a spouse, or a close friend or roommate who feels like family. Ideally, they will help you maintain a balanced perspective of your life as a whole based on a historical connection, rather than just the immediate view of a new mentor or counselor. They will also help you think through the impact of your changes on your family system. It is important to balance your development and professional focus with your family commitments.

**Professor or advisor:** Consider having a person who is an independent expert in the process of development. Most have undergone rigorous training or have significant experience in the field to support your development and success, and because they are independent, they are generally free of the natural bias held by family members, friends, and colleagues. On college campuses, there are professionals trained to work with students in their out of class experience. They are called "student affairs professionals" and often hold jobs in offices like student activities, the multicultural center, residence life, or the wellness center. And while faculty can sometimes seem intimidating to students, many are thrilled when a student makes a concerted effort to reach out for mentorship. Many faculty members love their work BECAUSE of the students they serve. Keep this in mind as you consider approaching someone to help you. Working with the right professor or professional staff member can be very valuable, can significantly accelerate the development process, and can help you overcome barriers. Sometimes personal improvement is difficult. If you are experience stress and/or anxiety about this process, you might consider seeking counseling services on or off campus. All colleges offer some sort of counseling services specifically designed for students and many services are offered at no cost, at least for the initial sessions.

**Willingness and ability to commit time to your development:** This is imperative. Ask those committed to supporting your development how to optimize your time together, and also discuss your mutual needs. The idea is that everyone should benefit from a clear understanding of how both to support the growth process and create healthy reciprocity. It will also be important to consider the time commitment you desire. Be willing to explore options that allow you to minimize the amount of time you request. You may consider creative options like volunteering for an organization that your mentor or support person is involved with. In this way, you can spend time with that person doing something that is important to him/her. This would allow you to learn directly and also support that person in meeting their objectives.

> *"A well thought-out critique of what you are doing is as valuable as gold"*
>
> —Elon Musk

It is important to know not only who to select, but also who to avoid. Keep in mind that there are many well-meaning people who would love to help, but, realistically, who are overcommitted and cannot provide the type of support you seek. Others may lack strong support skills, such as the ability to give open and honest feedback. If someone lacks the time or skills to provide helpful advice delivered in a supportive way, you should not include them. What you do not need during an intense development process is to waste time and energy with someone whose involvement could derail you.

## Accepting Feedback

How you react to feedback is critical to your success at this point. You are asking people to provide you input and feedback on your success.

- Know what type of feedback you want and ask for it clearly. Also if there is feedback you don't want, tell the person in advance. As an example, I could seek feedback on how I am perceived during meetings from a highly perceptive colleague. I may not ask him for feedback on the content of my statements because I have much greater expertise. So, I would remind him before we go into a meeting that I would really appreciate his feedback on how I am doing in meeting my goal of being more authentic. After the meeting I will ask for his feedback and thank him.

- When you receive feedback:

    - Listen attentively to the other person

    - Manage your emotions if the feedback is difficult to hear (you may need to step away to process for a while before continuing the conversation)

    - Consider carefully what has been said and identify what you can do to learn from what you heard

    - Ask for clarification or examples if you need

    - Thank them for their feedback and tell them how much you appreciate it

- If the feedback was not useful, suggest how they might change it to be more helpful to you. Be sure to acknowledge the effort they made in giving the feedback even if it was not exactly what you wanted

- Follow-up and tell them how you used the feedback to improve your effectiveness

Feedback is critical to developing yourself. How you accept and process the feedback will have a direct impact on other people's willingness to continue to give you feedback.

## Tools

The following worksheets are designed to help you connect your development action plan with the people who will help you accomplish these goals. They will fulfill different roles, ranging from encouragement and support to providing skilled expertise. You might also choose to include those who may be more directly impacted by the changes you are making. The more information you can provide during the process, the more likely they will be to support you or communicate their concerns to help you accomplish your goals. For an example, see how Anthony, Shelby, and Kelly approach the task.

## Real World Application

### Selecting Your Mentors

Carefully read the criteria and do the exercises. For each type of goal, write down as many specific people you know who would fit that role, even if you have not introduced yourself to that person yet. Think of family, friends, classmates, people in your residence hall, members of your student organizations, and co-workers. If you are looking for mentorship for a professional goal, consider professionals in a related field, or even professors who teach that. If you don't know many professionals, then you might consider finding an internship as a way to make connections.

After completing the worksheet, prepare to approach these people. If you already know them well, contact them as you normally would; however, if you have not introduced yourself, it is important to be a bit more careful and strategic. Look for an opportunity to run into them, contact them via social media or e-mail, or have a mutual friend introduce you if possible. LinkedIn is the best social media option to develop professional contacts for most professional fields. It is also critical to remember that as you link to professional contacts, your social media activities impact how others perceive you. In today's world, it is highly probable your online activities will be evaluated by potential employers and colleagues. You might consider doing a full "sweep" of your social media accounts to be sure that any information, photos, or videos posted are appropriate for professional contacts. Whether or not you believe it is fair or not, what you post on social media will impact how others perceive you, and could impact your future success.

### TABLE 5.1: SUPPORT TEAM WORKSHEET

| Goal | Type of Support I Need | Role | Skills/Knowledge or Other Criteria | Arrangement |
|---|---|---|---|---|
|  |  |  |  |  |
|  |  |  |  |  |
|  |  |  |  |  |
|  |  |  |  |  |
|  |  |  |  |  |

## Development Journey Continued

After creating their development plans, Anthony, Shelby, and Kelly are now evaluating who will help them implement their goals.

### SUPPORT TEAM WORKSHEET – ANTHONY

| Goal | Type of Support I Need | Role | Skills/ Knowledge or Other Criteria | Arrangement |
|------|------------------------|------|--------------------------------------|-------------|
| I have difficulty with active listening when I first meet someone and often cannot retain details from that first meeting | Family, Friends, Colleagues, Professors, Mentors | ▰ To make sure that I keep myself accountable for writing down important information | Acquired efficiency skills during my four years of college playing baseball since it required balancing time commitments to school, baseball and social events | I will make sure to maintain a complete list of tasks and time frames to assure all are completed by the due date on my timeline |
| Work on becoming more engaged as a lifelong learner and remaining curious about new ideas | Professional mentors, colleagues, professors | ▰ I will keep a running written daily calendar of events, people that I have met, the important information I have heard in discussions. I will seek feedback and repeat the information I hear from my customers and friends to make sure I fully understand what they have or are asking | Working for two separate internships in one summer really challenged me to retain information and learn about different aspects of business through individuals that I worked with | Make sure to keep accurate information regarding individuals, and specific information regarding situations and tasks to be completed. Keep an open mind about new ideas or areas of the job that I am less familiar with |
| I need to improve my self-motivation | Family, Friends, colleagues, Bosses, Mentors | ▰ Make sure that I am enthusiastic and upbeat about the work I am doing<br><br>▰ Become the best student and soon to be best employees that I can become | Take one task at a time and put 100% in each of the tasks<br><br>Use my achiever strengths and make lists and prioritize<br><br>Make every job as fun as I can using my natural curiosity and my positivity in order to stay on track and remain excited | Evaluate myself before and after every task to make sure that I put in all of the effort that I could<br><br>Set up monthly meetings with boss or professor to check progress and what more I can do to be the best asset to the company or university |

## SUPPORT TEAM WORKSHEET - SHELBY

| Goal | Type of Support I Need | Role | Skills/ Knowledge or Other Criteria | Arrangement |
|------|------------------------|------|-------------------------------------|-------------|
| Being open to new perspectives/ connect to being a better listener | Family, Friends, Colleagues/ Coworkers | ▬ Help me remain self-aware<br><br>▬ Provide instant feedback in conversations<br><br>▬ Let me know when I reach my goal | Excellent communication and listening skills<br><br>Know me well and are confident in giving me feedback/critiques | When I am talking to my support system, I will expect them to give me a nonverbal signal for when I am not listening to important information or other perspectives |
| Talking over people when they are speaking | Family, Friends | ▬ Provide instant feedback in conversations | Excellent communication and listening skills<br><br>Know me well and are confident in giving me feedback/critiques | My family and friends actually need to cut me off and tell me when I interrupt them and need to let them finish. This seems kind of counterintuitive, but I think in order for me to fix this behavior, I need to be corrected immediately in the moment |

## SUPPORT TEAM WORKSHEET - KELLY

| Goal | Type of Support I Need | Role | Skills/ Knowledge or Other Criteria | Arrangement |
|------|------------------------|------|-------------------------------------|-------------|
| Think more creatively in life (and more specifically in fashion) | Friends and fashion/creative project teams | ■ Learn different things from other creative people, especially those in the fashion industry<br><br>■ Gain experience and connections for my dream career<br><br>■ Consider other ways to tap into my creativity through writing, drawing, painting, etc | People who have rich experiences and broader vision of life and fashion | Everyday contact with friends/ connections and work with teams weekly on projects |
| Improve my ability to articulate my own ideas to people | Resources, feedback and encouragement from professional colleagues, mentor, supervisor, classmates | ■ Professionals and supervisors in workplace set good examples for me to learn speaking skills<br><br>■ Ask my mentors to help me capitalize on my strength of communication and realize that my fear of sharing my ideas verbally may just be that – fear; what I actually have to say is articulate and valuable to the organization if they can validate this in me, perhaps I can find the courage to improve<br><br>■ Recognize the small steps I take to improve and help me see it when I do well | People who are strong at speaking out in meetings and in larger groups and also willing to mentor and/or support my growth | View every meeting as a chance to observe and learn from the professionals/ supervisors<br><br>Ask friends/ colleagues to ask for my opinion during meetings<br><br>Ask for friends/ colleagues to give me feedback |
| Build on my ability to connect with others and work in teams | Recommenda- tions, feedback and encouragement from colleagues, mentor, supervisor, and classmates | ■ Introduce me to others<br><br>■ Recommend tools to help expand my network<br><br>■ Recognize when I do well with small connections I am able to make<br><br>■ Provide encouragement | People with strong networks and who are strong connectors | Schedule a weekly call for idea sharing with a couple of friends. Go to networking events such as conferences |

Once you determine your support team and their corresponding roles, you will want to figure out communication, timing, and expectations. This is the place to consider the kind of feedback you might expect from others to ensure you are making meaningful progress. This communication can provide you with invaluable information and feedback that is critical for your success. Since your plan is based on your own intuitive senses, the ongoing data should confirm your assumptions and serve as a feedback mechanism to refine your thinking.

The following are Communication Worksheets from Shelby, Anthony, and Kelly. You can use them as examples of how one may use communication when managing change both personally and within an organization.

### 5.2: COMMUNICATION PLANNING WORKSHEET – TEMPLATE

| Who | What to Communicate | What They Can Expect From You | What You Want From Them | How Often |
|-----|--------------------|-----------------------------|-------------------------|-----------|
|     |                    |                             |                         |           |
|     |                    |                             |                         |           |
|     |                    |                             |                         |           |

## COMMUNICATION PLANNING WORKSHEET – ANTHONY

| Who | What to Communicate | What They Can Expect From You | What You Want From Them | How Often |
|-----|--------------------|-----------------------------|------------------------|-----------|
| Family members and friends | How well am I balancing my time and retaining important information | I will continually improve my abilities to balance time in order to ensure total productivity and enhance my ability to retain information regarding customers, use timelines with my colleagues to complete projects and develop a stable base of consumers for my organization | I would like to make sure that they set aside time to talk about my improvements or personal changes that I need to work on and how I could accomplish those goals | I would like these meetings or phone calls to happen at least once or twice a week. The more I can be accountable, the faster I can demonstrate improvement in my personal goals |
| Colleagues and Professional mentor/ Professors | I would like to discuss more of the real life approaches and different ways to handle specific situations. It would be a continuous learning process to interact with my mentors | They can expect me to take notes on the information that they would be sharing with me. I will seek advice regarding how they have responded in certain situations to learn from their experience | As my mentor and teacher, I would like them to have time to share personal experiences so that I could learn from those who have already gone before me in the workplace | I would like to have a lunch meeting, meeting in their office or in the cafeteria at least once a week so I would be able to apply what I have learned the following week |

## COMMUNICATION PLANNING WORKSHEET – ANTHONY

| Who | What to Communicate | What They Can Expect From You | What You Want From Them | How Often |
|---|---|---|---|---|
| Family members (parents and brothers) | How well am I managing my personal life (i.e., health, finances, home, plan of personal improvement, etc.)?<br><br>How true am I remaining to my overarching vision and values? | I am continually improving my ability to manage the small details in life that are important, and to let go of the ones that are not<br><br>I am continually prioritizing the tasks and responsibilities I face, both personally and professionally<br><br>I am accomplishing my vision in the framework of my values | Time to discuss my areas of progress and needed improvement<br><br>Proactive accountability in the areas in which I am weak<br><br>Encouragement to let go of insignificant items and to focus my attention on the important ones | Weekly calls |
| Personal and professional mentors | How well am I managing my professional life (i.e., education, work experience, plan for professional improvement, etc.)?<br><br>How well am I prioritizing and managing multiple projects at the same time, and what are the results?<br><br>How true am I remaining to my overarching vision and values? | I am continually prioritizing the tasks and responsibilities I face, both personally and professionally<br><br>I am prioritizing and managing multiple projects at the same time which are delivering substantial impact collectively toward organizational goals<br><br>I am accomplishing my vision in the framework of my values | Time to discuss my areas of progress and needed development<br><br>Experience in managing complex situations and multiple projects at once within the same organization | Bi-weekly calls/meetings |
| Business partners | How am I doing in prioritizing and managing each of the projects for which I am responsible?<br><br>How well do these projects align in progressing toward accomplishing our shared vision, in the framework of our shared values? | Delivering excellent results for each of my projects which cumulatively creates progress toward our organizational goals<br><br>The same type of information that I am seeking from them, about their projects. Feedback on their progress<br><br>Unwavering commitment to accomplishing our shared vision in the framework of our shared values | Time to discuss my areas of progress and needed development<br><br>Time, resources, and flexibility to experiment and execute my projects in creative and unconventional ways | Daily meetings and correspondence |

## COMMUNICATION PLANNING WORKSHEET – SHELBY

| Who | What to Communicate | What They Can Expect From You | What You Want From Them | How Often |
|-----|---------------------|------------------------------|-------------------------|-----------|
| Family-My mom and brother | How is my tone? Do you feel valued in our conversations?<br><br>Am I appearing over-committed to my own ideas? | Self-correction when I realize I have not made a positive step to meet my goal<br><br>Asking questions and checking in when we talk | I need full honesty from my mom and my brother. They need to be unafraid to tell me what I sound like when I am communicating with them | Every time we talk. (phone, FaceTime, and in person when I visit home) |
| Friends | How is the volume of my voice? Can you tell I am consciously listening to what you say before I respond? | My friends can expect me to not get defensive (even if I feel like I should) when they give me feedback<br><br>Like my family, I will also continue asking questions and checking in when we talk | I need my friends to be candid in correcting me, but not cruel or hurtful. The friends I have in mind are brutally honest and can sometimes be a bit harsh in their feedback. I need careful, honest feedback from them | After a conversation or when they are feeling like I am interrupting too much in a conversation |
| Colleagues/ Coworkers | At work, do you feel comfortable talking to me in any situation? | Coworkers and colleagues can expect a change in my behavior that is slight, but appreciated. They can expect me to continue to value them and listen intently | I need my coworkers to answer my questions honestly and truthfully based on their interactions with me | I think with some coworkers I could do a daily check-in at the end of the day. I will ask others periodically during professional development time on Fridays |

## COMMUNICATION PLANNING WORKSHEET – KELLY

| Who | What to Communicate | What They Can Expect From You | What You Want From Them | How Often |
|-----|---------------------|------------------------------|-------------------------|-----------|
| Parents | Progress on goals and questions I have that they can help with | Ongoing communication and building a successful career and healthy life | Discuss how to improve my networking/ interpersonal skills, how to manage my personal finances, and any other questions I have | We contact through texting via cellphone and make phone calls often. No fixed schedule |
| Friends who are successful at work | How can I get more information on career advancement for job searching?<br><br>How can I improve my interview/ communication skills to impress the recruiters?<br><br>What are the most important things I must show and improve upon in work? | Discussing and displaying my progress in conversations<br><br>They can also expect me to help mentor them in the future or be available to support their goals | To learn how they think, what they do and why they are successful<br><br>To establish a strong professional relationship with them to expand my professional network | Daily, through talking, texting, and/ or email |
| Supervisors at my job | What should I learn to improve my ability in team environments?<br><br>How do I lead a project or finish a project independently?<br><br>How do I manage my time when I have a huge workload? | Be able to lead a group or project independently and deliver excellent and creative results<br><br>Be more efficient in work | To learn from their experience in leading projects and handling all kinds of issues<br><br>Resources/contacts for projects | Anytime during work |

## Real World Applications

### Internships – Ideal Professional Mentorship

If you're having difficulty finding a professional mentor, an internship is one of the best ways to do this, plus there are countless other benefits that an internship brings. Ideally, you do work for a company that aligns with your professional goals, while receiving feedback and mentorship from someone within the company. Other benefits may include financial rewards, valuable experience, additions to resume, letters of recommendation, networking and so much more. Before you start an internship, communicate your mentorship goals to your superiors/coworkers. Obtaining an internship may seem difficult and competitive, but it doesn't have to be if you take certain approaches.

While career fairs and job listing websites are a great way to get an internship at a "big name" company, they are the most competitive way. Consider this: for every "big name" company you see at a career fair, there may be a dozen small and local companies in your area that do the same thing. These smaller companies don't have the time or resources to recruit at a career fair or job website, and many of these companies don't even realize they need an intern. Do a search of companies in your area that do what you want to do, look on their Website for an e-mail address, and don't be afraid to politely reach out to them. Smaller companies can benefit from your help more, which increases their likelihood to accept you as well as give you more responsibility and hands-on experience. Another perk is that the owner of the company may have worked at a big name company in the industry for a long time, and is extremely skilled, experienced, and connected, which is why they are confident enough to start their own company. In summary, getting in internship in your desired industry is one of the best things you can possibly do while in college. Go get one!

## Innovative Leadership Reflection Questions

To help you develop your action plan, it is time to further clarify your direction using reflection questions. The questions for "What do I think/believe?" reflect your intentions. "What do I do?" questions reflect your actions. The questions "What do we believe?" reflect the culture of your organization (i.e., work, school, community), and "How do we do this?" questions reflect systems and processes for your organization. This exercise is an opportunity to practice innovative leadership by considering your vision for yourself and how it will play out in the context of your life. You will define your intentions, actions, culture, and systems in a systematic manner. If you are having difficulty defining a context because you aren't currently affiliated with an organization, you can choose to omit responses to those or use an organization that you aspire to join. Student organizations or student working contexts would be fine to consider.

Table 5.3 contains an exhaustive list of questions to appeal to a broad range of readers. A few will likely fit your own personal situation; focus on the ones that seem the most relevant. We recommend you answer one to three questions from each of the categories.

## TABLE 5.3: QUESTIONS TO GUIDE THE LEADER AND ORGANIZATION

**What do I think/believe?**

- What qualities do I want in the people I ask to support my personal change?
- What qualities will I eliminate from my current and future team?
- How do I think my change will impact those closest to me?
- Why would others spend their time and energy to help me develop?
- How much support do I expect from others?
- Am I making reasonable requests of those close to me?
- Am I looking for others who are making similar changes?
- Do I want people around me to change along with me?
- Because my development may be a very personal and even private choice, what am I willing to communicate to others?

**What do I do?**

- How do I determine and communicate the criteria for the right people to support me? "Right" includes personality traits, innate capabilities, skills, knowledge, time, and willingness.
- Once I know the criteria, who are the right people and how do I figure out which roles I would like them to take to support my success? How do I invite them to support this important personal transformation?
- Who do I ask to participate in my change?
- Who may become a barrier to my change? How do I mitigate their negative impact? What are immediate steps and longer-term actions?
- How do I ask for feedback? Am I clear about what information would be helpful to me and what information would not be helpful?
- How do I demonstrate that I genuinely appreciate the support others are providing?
- How do I communicate my need and desire for accurate feedback?
- What do I communicate when my situation and priorities change?

**What do we believe?**

- What are the social and cultural norms that dictate the type of support I should ask for and expect?
- How do we use my personal change as an opportunity to test new behaviors and demonstrate their positive impact on the group (professional organization, family, community)?
- What are our beliefs about who does the communicating? How much information do they share? How often? Do we solicit input or just convey information?
- What type of feedback will I seek from others to determine if they are supportive of my personal changes?
- Does our current school or team culture and approach to communicating support me in making the changes I am trying to make?

> **What do we do this?**
>
> ◢ How will I communicate? Who wants information? When? Through what medium? What are the key messages? How do I keep multiple supporters informed with the right amount of information at the right time to enhance buy-in and support for my behavioral change?
>
> ◢ What are the key skills and behaviors that both support my transformation and are necessary in my team? What are the gaps between my current support team and the team needed to support transformation?
>
> ◢ Do I have the right people available with the right skills and behaviors? Do I need to augment my support team with professionals such as a coach, therapist, spiritual advisor, clergy, colleague, or boss?
>
> ◢ What is the best combination of approaches for me to meet my support needs? Does this include professors, advisors, friends and/or family?
>
> ◢ What activities can we conduct to improve my degree of comfort with those supporting me?
>
> ◢ Am I communicating what supporters believe is important to them? Do they see the progress they hope to see?
>
> ◢ How do I communicate wins to stakeholders to sustain their reinforcement and energy?

We will now walk through Anthony's answers to one or two questions from each section of Table 5.3. Simply follow along with Anthony, Shelby, and Kelly to answer the questions for yourself, or select the questions that fit your current situation.

## Anthony's Responses to Reflection Questions

### What do I think/believe?

◢ **What qualities do I want in the people I ask to support my personal change?**

The critical qualities I would like to see in the people that support me are accountability and dedication to personal improvement. The three qualities that I would like from both my family and friends, and colleagues, professional mentors, and professors, are trustworthiness, truthfulness, and guidance. The reasons I chose those qualities is because I would want them to point out personal changes, and be able to trust that they would tell me when I need to change and be truthful about situations if I ask them for feedback. I also want them to have the ability to guide me in the direction that would make me successful in positive personal change. Being able to talk to professors and mentors who have graduated college, and have their own businesses makes it much easier to trust their judgment, and know that they will help guide me in a successful direction. I have had many professors who have given me their insight on different ways to approach studying, internships, and balancing time while playing baseball in college. Their openness to my asking for feedback made me feel as if they would be able to guide me in positive directions after I graduate.

## What do I do?

### ◢ Who do I ask to participate in my change?

I would ask that the people who are monitoring my changes participate with me since without their involvement in my growth process it would be more difficult to improve. Being so close to my family makes it easy for me to go to them for help and ask what they would do in certain situations, or how they would think through solutions to a problem. Attending a small college where you get to know your professors really well makes it easy to approach them as well with questions about classes, exams, personal problems, and also to get helpful tips in business. Participating in a number of leadership classes, listening to my professor's real life stories, examples and how she handled them is important to me. These illustrations will be able to help me think in a way that is logical and in a manner that I will need one day in the workplace.

## What do we believe?

### ◢ Do I have the right support to change the culture of our group to allow me to sustain the changes I am trying to make?

I believe that I do have the right support of people to help me with the changes that I need to make. My family is my main support system presently because I know they have already gone through college and both my parents have successful jobs which involve balancing their time between work and home. The importance of communication with others through meetings, projects that need completed or simply making sure that their employees are striving to be their best has been demonstrated to me through observing my parents in their workplace roles. I know that my parents hold high standards for themselves as I do for myself. This fact makes it easy for them to relate to where I want to go with my personal changes. Having professors/mentors with their own personal businesses and teaching the material to me is a great support system. Having mock interviews in class, real life situation descriptions of what I will face in the workplace, and key ways to organize myself to balance and remind myself about important information has been beneficial in my college career.

## How do we do this?

### ◢ What is the best combination of approaches for me to meet my support needs? Does this include hiring a coach or scheduling regular lunches with a trusted colleague?

I believe that the best combinations of approaches that I can take to meet my personal changes would be to have weekly meeting or phone calls with my family, friends, colleagues, professional mentors, and professors. This would be the best way because it would hold me accountable in short time frames such as a week instead of trying to do too much over a longer period of time. Being able to start with small traceable changes would be helpful. If progress is maintained on a weekly basis, and my support group notices the personal changes, then we would be able to move to once a month interaction. Having the support of my family and friends at a click of a button and having the relationship that I do with my professors I know that I am in the best support system that I could have to achieve success.

## Shelby's Responses to Reflection Questions

### What do I think/believe?

▰ **What qualities do I want in the people I ask to support my personal change?**

I need my support system to consist of people who are honest, trustworthy, and have excellent communication skills themselves. Honesty and trustworthiness go hand in hand for me. In any situation where you are seeking to change a behavior, the people supporting you need to be honest in their feedback and you need to trust them. I find it very important that my supporters also have qualities of being excellent communicators. They need to be the exemplar model for what I am striving for in my goal. I cannot trust someone who has poor communication skills to provide me with the feedback and tools to be better at communicating!

### What do I do?

▰ **Who do I ask to participate in my change?**

My mom and my brother would be the two family members I would call on for support. I talk to them the most and when I'm visiting home, I see them they most. From a family perspective, they can provide the most authentic feedback because they see me and talk to me a lot. I have two friends in mind, one who is also a co-worker, and they would be willing to participate in my change. They are two people who know me best as a person and in a professional context and they are unafraid to give me feedback about how I'm doing in any situation.

### What do we believe?

▰ **Do I have the right support to change the culture of our group to allow me to sustain the changes I am trying to make?**

Yes. This is my life, my change, and my goal, therefore, it has to work for ME. It's not selfish or self-centered to say this either. I am in charge of my changes and when given the authority to select my support group, I want what's best for me and the people who will help me sustain the changes I am striving to make.

## How do we do this?

■ **What is the best combination of approaches for me to meet my support needs? Does this include hiring a coach or scheduling regular lunches with a trusted colleague?**

I think open communication with all people involved will be the best approach to making my support really count in my change. Not that we need to sit down and have a group meeting about me, but just making sure I tell everyone the same thing and am communicating my goals eloquently to each person so they know exactly what I need and how I need it. Keeping my communication with each supporter streamlined and consistent in achieving my goal in the most efficient way possible.

## Kelly's Responses to Reflection Questions

## What do I think/believe/?

■ **What qualities do I want in the people I ask to support my personal change?**

Experience, honesty, and willingness to help.

I often chat with my parents and ask for advice on many things, especially how to manage my own finances and how to get along with others. They know me best, maybe even better than I know myself. I believe all the advice they give me is for my own good. They are always ready to give me general advice.

Also, I often contact some peers, mostly friends who have graduated and have already spent a few years in the workforce. From them I can get a clearer vision of how to improve myself step by step. They are more successful and skillful than I in some areas. They have richer experience in some areas of interest. They are outgoing, active, creative, and have a large professional network.

Supervisors and managers at work have rich experience in my specific area of expertise. I will be able to learn specific knowledge from them.

I also realize that I need to do a lot of this work on my own. Tapping into my natural strengths and abilities will help me build my own self-confidence. Asking for advice is good up until a point and then I need to see how I can solve challenges on my own, using my strengths.

■ **How do I think my change will impact those closest to me?**

I believe the knowledge and skills I learn from others will help me to greatly improve. In the future, my family, friends, and coworkers will be proud of my achievements. I will be happy to help others who need advice and help just like I was helped when I was in college. My change will also increase my capability, flexibility, and efficiency at work—and my team and projects will benefit from my change.

Since one of my key goals is to be financially self-sufficient, it will be important for me to build a reputation that allows me to advance in my career and succeed. This will impact my parents and family because they are helping support me right now.

## What do I do?

■ **Who may become a barrier to my change? How do I mitigate their negative impact? What are immediate steps and longer-term actions?**

My competitors (people who are competing with me for jobs and later for promotions) may be the biggest barrier to my change. When I am practicing and developing myself, my competitors may also be doing the same thing. I need to continue to excel to stand out. I need to balance myself and try to convert negative emotions into positive emotions and motivation. I will use my strength of positivity to do that. I will observe their performance during work, analyze their advantages and disadvantages, and focus on some specific skills to practice. In the long-term, my goal is not to defeat them, but to befriend them to increase my professional network and for all of us to be successful. I will also use my strength of individualization to see what strategies work for my competitors and how I can adapt those strategies to work specifically for me. I realize that I will not always be able to work exactly as my competitors do. They have used their strengths to be successful and I need to use my strengths in my own way for my success.

Other than competitors, I am a barrier to myself. There are so many personal reasons that could stop myself from development. The biggest is fear. I need to remind myself that I can be my authentic self and focus on building my strengths. People will appreciate what I have to offer if I can just be myself while also building important skills for my field. By monitoring myself, focusing on my strengths, and getting feedback, I can set up a plan to achieve long-term goals.

## What do we believe?

■ **What are the social and cultural norms that dictate the type of support I should ask for and expect?**

Because I am an international student and come from a country that has a totally different culture, I have to study American culture and norms to assimilate to society. I understand that networking is very important in the US, but the way we treat each other is so much different here than in my home country of China. In this situation, I will seek help from my local friends rather than my parents. They can usually give me very strong advice. I also had a brief interview with my supervisors and asked about fitting into a different society and some certain norms in work and social situations. If I want the best answers, I have to know what kind of questions I have, and who has the most experience. This helps me target the type of support I should ask for, and get the best advice. And while I realize that I will need to alter some ways in which I behave in order to accommodate the cultural customs in the US, I will also try to maintain the cultural values from China that are so important to me.

## How do we do this?

■ **What activities can we conduct to improve my degree of comfort with those supporting me?**

I believe communication is most important in improving my degree of comfort with those supporters. Through effective communication and by focusing on my strengths of communication, I can know their thoughts and become inspired by them. Healthy and continuous communication with supporters strengthens our understanding of each other, and it can strengthen our long-term relationship. A fixed, long-term, and positive relationship can create great support.

The other activity I would conduct is to show some of my strengths more often to others, while also seeking ways to improve. I have great relationship-building strengths like positivity and individualization (which helps me support my friends and those around me). If I can feel more confident letting people see my strengths, perhaps I can grow more quickly. More people will support you if you can show your good nature and see the benefits of supporting you. By improving my interpersonal skills, and myself, I can stand out among people and let others see my strength and value. If others think I am valuable, they would be happy and willing to support me.

## Build Your Team and Communicate

Now that you have seen the worksheets and read through the sample case narratives, it is time to complete the worksheets and answer the questions for yourself if you have not done so already. We encourage you to complete all of the exercises. Based on your support preferences, complete Table 5.1 (Support Team worksheet) and Table 5.2 (Communication Planning worksheet), then answer one to three questions from each section in Table 5.3.

This chapter serves to help you clarify your supporters and communication plan as you begin defining your feedback sources. This is the plan that will provide you with expertise, emotional support, buy-in, and feedback for your development. While creating a communication plan may seem extraneous, never underestimate the value of both emotional and moral support, and communication to and from those who will be affected by your changes. This could be as simple as talking to your spouse or family about the way your changing routine may impact them, while letting them know you appreciate their willingness to be flexible.

**What do I think/believe?**

**What do I do?**

## What do we believe?

## How do we do this?

# CHAPTER 6
## Step 5: Take Action

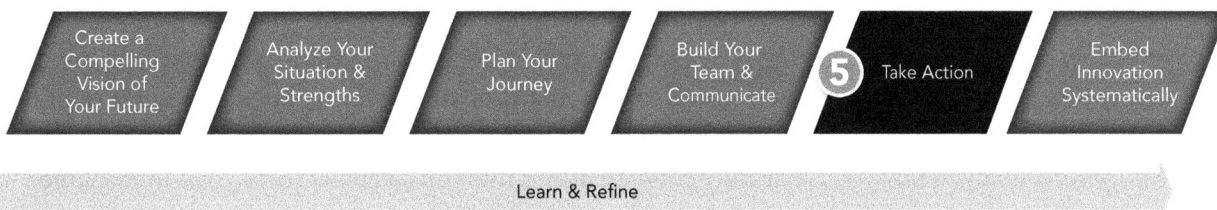

| Create a Compelling Vision of Your Future | Analyze Your Situation & Strengths | Plan Your Journey | Build Your Team & Communicate | 5 Take Action | Embed Innovation Systematically |

Learn & Refine

Now that you have created a plan to become an innovative leader and have defined your support team, it is time to take action. Your plan should spell out which actions you want to take, how often, and who can support your progress.

As you begin realizing your vision, you may start to identify challenges to your growth and development. Barriers are simply a normal part of any transformative process; we have provided a number of useful tools to help pinpoint and navigate them successfully.

An important part of your success is believing that you can make progress and sustain growth in your leadership ability. You have developed a strong foundation by creating a compelling vision and analyzing unique challenges and opportunities to determine what actions you need to take to achieve your goals.

Be aware that this stage can take tremendous focus and energy. Many people stumble here, especially when the change process becomes difficult and the demands of balancing life requirements take on greater urgency. Think, for example, of how many times you may have started an exercise program at a gym, but did not follow your plan to go there as frequently as you had intended. Implementing your plan requires a deep commitment to your growth and also an understanding of the barriers you will face based on your personality type or history with implementing change. As barriers surface, you have the ability to remove them or modify your course with the support of your team.

> *"Sometimes unforeseen events stress me out because I feel like my personal and leadership development will be ruined. Exams and projects would overwhelm me and I felt like I didn't have time to work on myself. Then I thought about my overall goal, or even the altruistic/ purpose related dimension of why I want to lead and affect change. It helped me manage my time very carefully, and re-evaluate behaviors and commitments in my life that were distracting me from my true purpose."*
>
> —Eric Philippou

With this in mind, allow yourself some flexibility in your development process instead of viewing your plan as fixed. See your plan as an initial starting point, or a working hypothesis about how you will develop. With that perspective, you can better use the challenges you face as a way to provide feedback on your original hypothesis and modify it as you go along. In other words, rather than viewing these obstacles as threats, you have the opportunity to naturally incorporate them as mechanisms for fine-tuning. For each challenge you face, carefully consider the unique learning opportunity and how to use it to help you implement your plan. Since personal development is a lifetime journey, you will have many opportunities to face these challenges and take corrective actions.

Lastly, your support team will play a crucial role in helping to make the plan sustainable. They will offer you input and feedback as well as encouragement during times when you struggle. Even though you specifically chose the changes and goals within your plan, it is often still helpful to have a built-in system of accountability. When you run into inner resistance and difficulty, connect with someone who will remind you that you are already competent and that you can meet these goals in the same way you have met many other challenges.

## Tools

The following worksheet helps you to anticipate barriers and mitigate them while implementing your action plan. You can refer to the completed case sample worksheets as examples.

**TABLE 6.1: BARRIERS: ACTION PLANNING WORKSHEET**

| Category | Barrier | Impact of Barrier | How to Remove or Work Around using strengths | Support I Need to Remove or Work Around |
|---|---|---|---|---|
| In my thinking | | | | |
| In my behavior | | | | |
| In our beliefs | | | | |
| In how we do things | | | | |

## Development Journey Continued

When we last met Anthony, he was building his support team and defining how he wanted to communicate. His responses will be followed by Shelby and Kelly.

**BARRIER ACTION PLANNING WORKSHEET – ANTHONY**

| Category | Barrier | Impact of Barrier | How to Remove or Work Around using strengths | Support I Need to Remove or Work Around |
|---|---|---|---|---|
| In my thinking | Sometimes I am an over-thinker, or seek too much input or information in trying to reach a decision | This could cause me not to think clearly and could cause me to cloud my judgment | I need to be aware that my learner strength can cause me to keep learning and not move toward a decision fast enough. I can use my competition and achiever strengths to be sure that I am executing the decision making process efficiently | Family/friends, professorial mentors, colleagues, and professionals in the work force |
| In my behavior | I like to remain active and always have to be doing something to keep me busy. I also like to be challenged in many different ways during tasks, and sometimes simple or menial tasks just need to get done. I have trouble motivating through those at times. I can also get caught up in trying to find the "perfect" solution to tough challenges which can take extra time and hold me back | Extra time to complete tasks and a lack of motivation for those tasks I am less engaged with | I can work around this problem by managing or balancing my time to make sure that I do not spend too much time in certain situations. My achiever strength can help me with this. And I can tap into my competition strength to work through the tough challenges faster by imagining that I am racing a clock or another person to finish first | Family/friends, professorial mentors, colleagues, and professors |

| Category | Barrier | Impact of Barrier | How to Remove or Work Around using strengths | Support I Need to Remove or Work Around |
|----------|---------|-------------------|---------------------------------------------|------------------------------------------|
| In our beliefs | Not being able to relax and enjoying down time from activities | Stress developed from having too much on my plate at one time for tasks to be completed<br><br>My achiever strength can become "workaholic" if I allow it to | Deciding on a more specific prioritization of tasks<br><br>Completing tasks before taking on new ones. Making sure that I am also trying to "achieve" balance and stress reduction activities in my life. Focusing my achiever on exercise and healthy habits | Family/friends, professorial mentors, colleagues, and professors |
| In how we do things | At one time or another we are all overwhelmed by taking on more tasks than we can handle at one time. The famous quote "There are not enough hours in the day" applies to both me and my family, and me and my girlfriend. We are not always a good influence on each other in this way | The problem with this is that we, as a family, commit to tasks that take up our own time that could be spent on other opportunities. This will become a challenge if we do not make time to provide one another with feedback. Perhaps I need my support system to commit to these goals along with me, to the extent they are willing | I know that I need to learn to say "no" more often when the activity isn't something I really want to do or something that won't benefit me. I like helping people every moment that I get but, I need to step back sometimes and see if I have the time to take on another task. My family will, hopefully, commit to this with me and support me in these decisions by asking good questions about my choices | Family/friends, professorial mentors, colleagues, and professors |

## BARRIER ACTION PLANNING WORKSHEET – SHELBY

| Category | Barrier | Impact of Barrier | How to Remove or Work Around using strengths | Support I Need to Remove or Work Around |
|---|---|---|---|---|
| In my thinking | This is just who I am..." <br><br> "I shouldn't have to change!" | My stubbornness could inhibit my ability to even try and make a change | Concentrating on my strength in *Communication* and *Developer*. I think it will be important to turn *Developer* toward myself instead of only focusing on developing others | I need to check myself! I can't get caught up in my own crazy thoughts. I need to let things happen and relax |
| In my behavior | Getting really excited in conversations and around others <br><br> Making sure I consider all alternatives and the perspectives of others in conversations | Excitement and zeal is great! But getting too wrapped up in it and not being able to "bring it back" will impact my development | I need to harness my strength, *Woo* and not let it get the best of me. Winning Others Over (WOO) is something that comes naturally for me and people love people with energy and vivacity. I need to make sure I keep it at a loveable level | Friends and family who are supporting me need to value my *Woo*, but know when I need to harness the *Woo* and tell me |
| In our beliefs | "Change is hard..." | Being open minded and willing to make change(s) in my life including my thinking is a huge asset in growth | Although *Adaptability* was not in my top 5 strengths, I believe I am quite good at adapting to situations, changes, and different things happening in life | Sometimes when I am feeling discouraged or can feel myself slipping back into a negative mindset about change, I can do something very simple, like read a motivational quote, or do something deeper like journal and write about how I'm feeling and things become more clear |
| In how we do things | Change needs to happen, change is good, we need to embrace it wholeheartedly and not with a frown and beaten down approach | Not embracing the change is pointless for this exercise! We must be all in | Being determined and focused will drive the force for "how we do things" | I need a united front that is ready to move onward in the achievement of my goal! When we are on the same page and working together, we'll be good to go |

## BARRIER ACTION PLANNING WORKSHEET – KELLY

| Category | Barrier | Impact of Barrier | How to Remove or Work Around using strengths | Support I Need to Remove or Work Around |
|---|---|---|---|---|
| In my thinking | My fear of being laughed at, not fitting in, and not being liked | It stops me from speaking and acting. I hide many ideas | I will continue to realize that I actually have a strength of communication! I will focus on when I have been courageous in the past and remind myself that I am capable of overcoming my own challenges | I will talk to my mentor and ask that he/she supports the development of my strength of communication. I may need to be reminded from time to time that it is a STRENGTH. This not only helps me release pressure, but also can encourage me to move forward |
| In my behavior | Compared to others, I am not as active and aggressive. I am not always the first one to speak out or act, and always wait for others to initiate | It is a very bad habit that can stop me from being an opinion leader and therefore lose attention from others | Tell myself that my opinions matter and draw on my courage to speak up more. Realize that my strength of Strategic can actually allow me to see the best solution, sometimes before others see it. By inserting my opinion, I could actually be benefitting the team | Following a coworker or leader who can inspire me to share opinions and speak up more. Learn from his/her actions and practice |
| In our beliefs | We always subconsciously fall into common thinking: to do as others do | This prevents us from showing our own talent/ creativity. This is safe and low-risk thinking, but may prevent us from potential growth | Understand who I am, what talents I have and what I want to prove. Understanding myself is the prerequisite of deciding what I can and will do | Observe and conclude my behavior from each group activity. Listen to peers/family/mentors and other people. From their advice, I understand what my image is to others, and improve my strengths/overcome my weaknesses |
| In how we do things | In my internship and classes— the system requires planning so others can manage their schedules in conjunction with mine | Every time after failing to do what I had planned, I feel upset and lose confidence. That prevents me from carrying out my thinking and showing my talents to others | Identify what keeps me from meeting my plans like watching too much TV and lacking time management skills | Ask for feedback from close friends/peers/ group members on their recommendations and also how I am doing at causing them problems because of my scheduling challenges |

## Real World Application

### *Create a Barrier Log*

Review your responses for the Barrier Action Planning Worksheet and create a spreadsheet document. Label the first column "Barrier". Move one column to the right, and label the next five columns, from left to right, "Attempt #1", "Attempt #2", and so on. In the column labeled "Attempt #1", write how you plan to overcome the corresponding barrier, using the response you put for the Barrier Action Planning Worksheet and explaining how you will use your strengths. If you fail on the first attempt, write a new or refined way to overcome that barrier, plus what you did wrong in the previous attempt and other strengths you can incorporate in your log, in the Attempt #2 section, and continue this process until you eventually overcome the barrier. On the attempt where you finally succeed, highlight that box in green. As new barriers rise, add them to the log; however, after you complete a barrier, it is critical that you keep it on the log and do not delete it!

This barrier log will be very useful because you will be able to track what did and did not work in order to overcome a barrier. You will likely come across barriers that are similar to previous ones, so knowing what worked (and what didn't work) in advance, making the barrier easy to overcome. As time goes on, and you begin to see a long list of old barriers with green boxes, signifying success, your confidence in overcoming barriers will increase. It may be grueling to keep adding more attempts because you keep failing, but understand the that only true failure is failure to try.

Feel free to include barriers outside of the leadership development process, such as academic, social and even health barriers. Save this document in a cloud storage service for both safety and convenience. Update it on a regular basis. Also, if one of your mentors from the Build Your Team section is an "equal", or someone in the same situation as you, have that person make a barrier log and share logs with each other online or during meetings, suggesting strengths the other has that may help them overcome barriers.

## Innovative Leadership Reflection Questions

To help you develop your action plan, it is time to further clarify your direction using reflection questions. The questions for "What do I think/believe?" reflect your intentions. "What do I do?" questions reflect your actions. The questions "What do we believe?" reflect the culture of your organization (i.e., work, school, community), and "How do we do this?" questions reflect systems and processes for your organization. This exercise is an opportunity to practice innovative leadership by considering your vision for yourself and how it will play out in the context of your life. You will define your intentions, actions, culture, and systems in a systematic manner.

Table 6.2 contains a thorough list of questions to appeal to a broad range of readers. You will likely find some that best fit your own personal situation; focus on those that seem the most relevant. We recommend you answer one to three questions from each of the categories. As a reminder, you may want to return to your values statement in Chapter 2 as a reminder when you complete the section on what do I think/believe.

## TABLE 6.2: QUESTIONS TO GUIDE THE LEADER AND ORGANIZATION

### What do I think/believe?

- To become more effective, what do I need to change about how I see myself or the world?
- Including beliefs, what do I need to let go of to make these changes?
- What do I see as my individual role? How does this role allow me to fit in different organizations, including my family?
- How can I benefit from my own personal growth and development?

### What do I do?

- How do I request clear and concise feedback that allows me to grow and supports the growth of others?
- How do I determine what I am ready to change within myself and what additional support I require for those changes I am resisting?
- What help am I willing to request? Am I investing appropriate time and/or resources to support my growth? Is the commitment I am making to my personal change consistent with the results I expect to receive?
- What creative solutions can I find to increase my personal awareness? Do I track my performance against my goals using logs or reflection activities?
- How will I identify times when my own behavior undermines my success? What will I do if I find my own behavior undermines my success?
- How do I encourage "bad news" as well as good from my support team?
- Am I looking for opportunities to visibly demonstrate my progress as my development process unfolds?
- What am I doing to retain my support team as time goes on?
- How do I manage my transformation over time? How do I focus on accomplishing my daily tasks while concurrently focusing sufficient time on my vision and goals?
- What feedback do I seek that will allow me to correct, redirect, or recalibrate my behavior and feel motivated to make the necessary changes?

### What do we believe?

- How will my changes impact my ability to be successful based on the organization's reward system, given its values, goals, and culture?
- Does our culture support the behavioral traits I am trying to develop?
- How can we connect prior learning successes to my current development effort? How can we use prior success to reinforce our ability to navigate current growth goals?

### How do we do this?

- What processes do we have that may serve as barriers to my developing in the way I would like? Am I in a position to remove these barriers? If I cannot remove the barriers, how will I navigate around them?
- What early warning signs can I track to let me know what impact my behavioral changes have on others? What indicators will alert me before any significant issues arise?
- How do my changes fit into the current reward and grading system? If there are misalignments, what will I do to navigate the barriers and challenges?
- Have I clearly articulated the changes I want to make and asked for the support of those around me?
- What communication processes do we use to provide timely feedback? How will these impact me during my development? How will my development impact others?
- What is the organization doing to measure, communicate, and fund my development and activities?

When we last met Anthony, he was building his support team and defining how he wanted to communicate. We will now walk through Anthony's answers to one or two questions from each section of Table 6.2. Simply follow along with Anthony to answer the questions for yourself or select the questions that fit your current situation.

### Anthony's Responses to Reflection Questions

### What do I think/ believe?

■ *What do I see as my individual role? How does this role allow me to fit in different organizations, including my family?*

My individual role can be identified as someone who never hesitates to help others and to learn as much as I can from every interaction in my life. I believe these individual roles will help me fit into different organizations because group collaboration and helping others is a key aspect of successful business. Not being self-centered and always willing to share ideas to help guide others or help the organization is a key to fitting in. When my family asks me to do something or help, I do not hesitate. I just do it because I care about, and will do anything for, them.

### What do I do?

■ *What feedback do I seek that will allow me to correct, redirect, or recalibrate my behavior and feel motivated to make the necessary changes?*

What I value above all in feedback is honesty. Feedback from those that I respect is critical for making needed changes in behavior. Developing a network of individuals that I can trust to be honest with me will allow a positive feedback loop to be created for change. Even as a young child when I would do something wrong my parents used immediate feedback to change inappropriate behavior.

### What do we believe?

■ *How will my changes impact my ability to be successful based on the organization's reward system, given its values, goals, and culture?*

Positive changes will impact and help me be successful my entire life. Making gradual positive changes will assist my organization to grow by establishing a positive loop to challenge the status quo of the company. Positive feedback will allow me to balance time to work toward organizational goals and objectives. Change ability will be tested more when I enter the working world. Balancing time is a critical part of life and I will continue to work and increase efficiency at balancing tasks.

Retaining information is another critical enhancement that I am working on changing. Being able to retain information will remain important for organizational success as a soon to be graduating student.

## How do we do this?

■ *Have I clearly articulated the changes I want to make and asked for the support of those around me?*

I believe that I have articulated the changes that I would like to enhance, and with my support system I believe that it very achievable. Honesty and trustworthiness of my support group and my willingness to work on enhancing my behavioral changes is a good starting point. Being able to trust the support system that surrounds me will only make it easier for me and my organization to succeed. I will need to make a conscious effort to communicate regularly and follow my communication plan. I realize that as we get busy, we may focus on the most urgent needs and forget to focus on one another's development.

## Shelby's Responses to Reflection Questions

## What do I think/believe?

■ *What do I see as my individual role? How does this role allow me to fit in different organizations, including my family?*

I have to be the leader for the changes in my life. My individual role is to be the leader and to take the feedback I am given. As a leader, I have to be fluid in how I go from organization to organization and group to group, taking all of the information I receive and compartmentalizing it into pieces that will contribute to my success.

## What do I do?

■ *Do I surround myself with others who are focused on their personal changes so that I have a reinforcement system?*

I have a very small group of people around me who are focused on personal changes and personal growth. I want to keep those people close and let them know that I need them as reinforcement in my life. I will let them know that I will reciprocate with the same support.

## What do we believe?

■ *How will my changes impact my ability to be successful based on the organization's reward system, given its values, goals, and culture?*

Simply going through these steps to make a detailed, well-designed plan will positively impact my success throughout life. Now that I have the tools and the practice with creating a plan when I need to make a change, I will feel more confident the next time I go about this process. Planning for change is a transferable skill that can be used in the workplace, in my personal life, and when I am leading others through change.

## How do we do this?

■ *Have I clearly articulated the changes I want to make and asked for the support of those around me?*

Yes! I feel confident that if someone asked me what I was working on in my life, I could provide a clear, well-articulated plan for what my goal is. The planning stages are some of the most important pieces of making change and it's so important that I and also my support system can communicate what changes I want to make.

## Kelly's Responses to Reflection Questions

## What do I think/believe?

■ *How can I benefit from my own personal growth and development?*

I believe this is a common thought process that is inherited from previous generations in China: the bird out of group will be shot, which leads many people to fall into a common mentality. This is an old saying that our people have believed for thousands of years. Many traditional people today still believe in it to avoid any danger or unexpected bad result. However, I know that this may prevent me from showing my talent and cannot bring me any outstanding achievements.

I didn't realize this problem until I entered the third year of college. There were many group studies, case competitions, and club activities. I now understand how important being an active opinion leader is—it gives me confidence, a sense of accomplishment, and improves my leadership skills. After being brought up in a culture of moderation, I decided to overcome this challenge. I believe I can show and find out more of my strengths, gain more skills and eventually acquire different skill sets. My development will be seen and can bring me many achievements.

Breaking the common mentality means to start a new journey, a journey to explore myself. I may see the world differently and more actively than I used to see it. And I believe the benefit from my own growth will positively influence my life and allow me to achieve my vision.

## What do I do?

- ### *How do I request clear and concise feedback that allows me to grow and supports the growth of others?*

I would choose one peer and one supervisor for feedback; in other events and activities, I would choose people who are close, have nice relationships with me and have worked with me for a long time. I do not go to people who seem indifferent to me, but I will try to improve our relationship first.

- ### *How do I encourage "bad news" as well as good from my support team?*

I think "bad news" is somehow more important than good news when you are trying to improve something, like a project or yourself. I do not avoid or ignore bad news because I want to know what we are not doing well enough so that we can do better. The bad news is the key that I can use to unlock my or my team's abilities and skill. It is even more terrible if I cannot know my weakness, which doesn't mean that I am infallible, but actually means I cannot see loopholes underneath. One can't improve anything that he/she doesn't see.

Comparably, I will maintain my strengths through positive feedback.

## What do I believe?

- ### *Does our culture support the behavioral traits I am trying to develop?*

There are still many people believing that the common mentality is safer than being aggressive. But my family supports me being aggressive and standing out. This is one of the reasons that they sent me thousands of miles away to study abroad and sacrificed seeing me often. The conservative culture does have its own benefits, but it does not apply in every situation.

I want to break this barrier because I don't want to fall into the same, simple life as many other students in my culture do: study hard to get high GPA and then get into a bank or take a civil servant exam for a stable life, get married and give birth to babies, bring up children and retire. This common lifestyle is desired by many people in my culture, but not by me. I want to explore my value, my dream, and enjoy a different life by developing myself to a new level.

- ### *How can we connect prior learning successes to my current development effort? How can we use prior success to reinforce our ability to navigate current growth goals?*

I joined a few student clubs when I was freshman, but I didn't go to the activities consistently or contribute any effort. At the end I thought the club was not helping my self-development at all. But the real problem was not the clubs, it was me–I was shy and afraid to put myself out of my comfort zone. When I started my internship in the summer of my sophomore year, I learned how to cooperate with others and work as a team. I got confirmation of my success when my manager told me that after I had joined the team, the sales of the product that I promoted for months had increased due to my effort. I gained confidence in myself since that excellent experience. I then applied my previous success to my next club activities and work. The cumulative experience and success from each activity and job made me who I am today. I reflect on my performance every time to find out the direction of my future path. Plus, I have realized that focusing on my strengths can lead to greater success for myself and for my team.

## How do we do this?

■ *What communication process do we use to provide timely feedback? How will this impact me during my development? How will my development impact others?*

I usually ask for others' opinions immediately when problems appear. That way I can adjust my direction and behavior immediately in order to make quick changes. In some situations, when everyone is busy, like at work, I would not bother him or her every time I have problems unless the problem is urgent. I use break times to communicate with others for feedback on my current progress. And after each project is done, I will ask for feedback from my supervisor or peers as well. Choosing a good time, like lunchtime, is important and could affect others' feedback.

Timely feedback helps me to know what I have done well and what I need to do more next time. And my growth will lead and encourage others who are seeking self-improvement too. Lastly, I think that reflecting on how I used my strengths in each successful situation will help me realize that I am using my strengths regularly and improving them.

## Process of Taking Action

Now that you have seen the worksheets and read through the narratives from Anthony, Shelby, and Kelly, it is time to complete the worksheets and answer the questions. We encourage you to complete all of the exercises and answer one to three reflection questions from each section in Table 6.2. This process serves to help you clarify what your barriers to success are, and how you will manage or remove them.

This chapter summarizes the basics for identifying barriers to successfully accomplish your goals as described in your plan. It also asks you to monitor the systems you put into place to measure your success and take corrective action. The next chapter will walk you through the process of ensuring that the changes you make are sustainable.

**What do I think/believe?**

**What do I do?**

## What do we believe?

**How do we do this?**

# CHAPTER 7

## Step 6: Embed Innovation Systematically

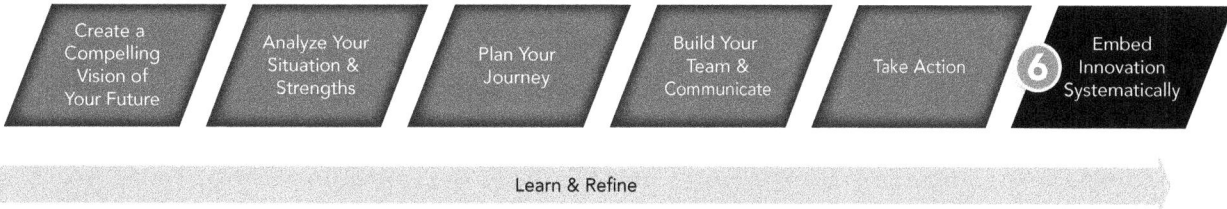

| Create a Compelling Vision of Your Future | Analyze Your Situation & Strengths | Plan Your Journey | Build Your Team & Communicate | Take Action | 6 Embed Innovation Systematically |

Learn & Refine

Congratulations! You have made it to the final chapter in your development process. You are now ready to shift from implementing your plan as something with a discrete end to considering how you will integrate these changes into your lifestyle going forward. We suggest you view your leadership development as an ongoing process rather than something to check off the to-do list. Given the volume of change we are facing now and expect to face in the future, continual development is a must simply to stay current. In this light, you can begin asking yourself, "What support can I put into place to stay on track? How can I gain additional benefits from ongoing practice?"

To maintain momentum, it is critical to retain a sense of urgency and minimize any complacency that may come from early success. Be aware that it is easy to stray from your goals if you declare success based on your early results, especially when other areas of your life tug at your time and attention. One helpful shift in thinking is to see the actions you are taking as practice rather than completion. You are practicing your leadership skills in the same fashion that a professional athlete practices a particular sport. The most successful athletes are constantly working to improve, even though they may already be the best in the world. This is why many of them remain successful over a long period of time. You will need to consider a long-term commitment to activities that foster success and help maintain your momentum.

> *"There was a lot of trial and error for me—similar to the mindset of the scientist. While the growth from this was incremental and slower than I wanted, each minor tweak adds up, and you get closer and closer to the ideal routine each time, making growth easier each time."*
>
> —Eric Philippou

So, ask yourself, "When I see progress, what will keep me motivated to continue practicing? I need some reminder that my progress is a result of engaged practice, and my performance is likely to suffer if I do not maintain proper focus."

At this point, you may want to re-evaluate your goals and begin raising the bar. You will need to balance long-term practice that sustains progress with identifying your next developmental focus or goals.

Altogether, this step invites you to be more conscious of actions as well as tangible barriers, and to identify the elements in your life that support the continual realization of your goals. Also, examine the events and relationships that interfere with your vision and goals. It is critical to remove as many barriers as possible and to stop behaviors that no longer align with your development goals. Remember that perseverance is key. Much of the research on leadership development suggests that it is a lifetime practice, not a short-term goal. You must be in learning-mode in all new situations—and new people will challenge you in new ways. Leadership is not a solo act. It is relational. And as you work with different teams, different personalities, and people who behave in different ways, you will need to re-evaluate your own perspective and behavior.

The overall objective in this chapter is to understand your habits and choices, and to confirm they are aligned with your long-term goals.

## Tools

Below is a table you can use to capture and track your progress. For many people, the simple act of recording their progress in writing helps maintain their commitment. Use the following worksheet to help track your progress against each of your goals. If you would like to see a sample, review the responses from Anthony, Shelby, and Kelly.

**TABLE 7.1 PERSONAL TRANSFORMATION ACTIVITY/PRACTICE LOG TEMPLATE**

| Goal | Action | Record Actual Performance | Expected Impact | Priority | Measure | Progress | Feedback from Whom |
|------|--------|---------------------------|-----------------|----------|---------|----------|--------------------|
|   | 1. |   |   |   |   |   |   |
| 1 | 2. |   |   |   |   |   |   |
|   | 3. |   |   |   |   |   |   |
|   | 4. |   |   |   |   |   |   |
| 2 | 5. |   |   |   |   |   |   |
|   | 6. |   |   |   |   |   |   |
|   | 7. |   |   |   |   |   |   |
| 3 | 8. |   |   |   |   |   |   |
|   | 9. |   |   |   |   |   |   |

## Anthony's Development Journey Continued

When we last met Anthony, he was taking action on his development plan. Anthony will now walk through his worksheets and journal entries for embedding change systematically.

### PERSONAL TRANSFORMATION ACTIVITY/PRACTICE LOG – ANTHONY

| Goal | Action | Record Actual Performance | Expected Impact | Priority | Measure | Progress | Feedback From Whom |
|---|---|---|---|---|---|---|---|
| 1 | 1. I have difficulty with active listening when I first meet someone | Day/Weekly self-checks | I will have a written daily calendar of events and people that I have met and the important information I have heard from them | 1 | To make sure that I keep myself accountable for writing down important information | Some improvement based on feedback and gauge how the improvement is impacting my goal | Family, friends, colleagues, professors, mentors |
| | 2. Often cannot retain details from that first meeting | Day/Weekly self-checks | I will have weekly meeting with a trusted colleague and mentor for feedback on improved active listen skill development | 2 | The weekly meetings will provide feedback | I am getting feedback on my consistent improve-ment | |
| 2 | Work on building my learner strength by increasing my curiosity about topics I am not familiar with | Will continue to improve every opportunity I can and make sure to have monthly checks | I will make sure that when I graduate and move on to the workplace to keep learning as much as I can and never stop being a student | 1 | I will make sure to make a list of new information that I learned for the week and make sure to revisit that information often to learn new ideas and improve | Always a work in progress | Myself, family, colleagues, and mentors |
| 3 | Focusing my Achiever strength to keep track of my priorities and use my Competition strength to stay motivated when I am less interested in a task. If I imagine myself competing with someone or against myself, I can motivate better to get it done | Will continue to improve every opportunity I can and make sure to have monthly checks | Try to remain enthusiastic and upbeat about the work I am doing, and try new strategies around my competition strength to stay motivated<br><br>Become the best student and soon-to-be best employee possible | 1 | Take one task at a time and put 100% in each of the tasks<br><br>Use my Competition and Achiever strengths to stay on track and remain engaged with tasks ahead of me | Always a work in progress | Family, friends, colleagues, bosses, mentors |

## PERSONAL TRANSFORMATION ACTIVITY/PRACTICE LOG – SHELBY

| Goal | Action | Record Actual Performance | Expected Impact | Priority | Measure | Progress | Feedback From Whom |
|---|---|---|---|---|---|---|---|
| 1 | Being open to new ideas and perspectives from others | Self-check and working with supporters daily/weekly | Others will feel heard and appreciated and I will take more informed action | 3 | Feedback that I am open to new points of view | I am seeing some improvement | Friends and family |
| 2 | Talking over people in conversations | Self-check and working with supporters daily/weekly | By allowing people to finish speaking and by paying attention to "turn taking" people will actively engage in meaningful conversation and my input will have greater impact | 1 | I can measure my progress by asking people I talk to if they felt like they were valued and listened to in our conversation | Improvement necessary and making slow and steady progress | Friends and family |

## PERSONAL TRANSFORMATION ACTIVITY/PRACTICE LOG – KELLY

| Goal | Action | Record Actual Performance | Expected Impact | Priority | Measure | Progress | Feedback From Whom |
|---|---|---|---|---|---|---|---|
| 1 | Speak aloud in group meetings or in work when I have new ideas | I spoke out in a meeting recently with a new idea. I was nervous but it was okay | (For all goals) Become a team and opinion leader step by step, be able to contribute good ideas to many projects and success, and be respected by others for my work, and not superficial things.

My strengths and my creativity are confirmed by others | 1 | Increase number of times I speak in groups, contribute ideas, and get response from group

How often I find myself stopping or being afraid of what others think, and how I react when it happens

Measure how much time I spend thinking about this

To gain confidence in my strengths, I will also track when I am using them in each activity

How nervous I become in situations where I speak aloud, and how effective I am in speaking situations | Slow progress because there are fewer group meetings recently | Supervisors, peers, close friends, and family |
|  | Overcome the weakness that I care too much about what other people think of me | Understand social acceptance is part of low leadership abilities |  |  |  | I focus more on my work, and less on fashion and looking the best at work, or being the most well-liked. My work has shown improvement; I still dress well, but with less worry involved | Myself, mainly. And if I am receiving fewer compliments on things like my clothes and more compliments on my work |
|  | Improve speech skills | Read words aloud when I am alone. I am counting the number of times I speak confidently in groups |  |  |  | I am still a little nervous but I push myself to speak out, and I get less nervous each time, which lets me speak better | My peers in situations in which I speak out. If they consistently understand my ideas, it is positive feedback |

| | | Manage different projects individually | I was successfully able to manage three projects and complete all of them on time | I will do well on my projects. My efforts will not go unnoticed and I will gain more complex and exciting projects | 4 | Increase the number of projects I can do, increase their complexity, and decrease the time required to complete them | Slow progress, but consistent improvement | Ask supervisors for feedback and advice on project progress, ask peers for ideas. My mother will be very helpful in giving advice at work because she is very experienced in managing projects |
| 2 | | Put effort in details and manage time spent on it | After I complete some work I double check each detail before submitting it to my boss or my professor | | 5 | Finding fewer mistakes when I correct my work | I keep finding mistakes, perhaps because I think about details after the project, and not while I'm doing the project | |
| | | Identify the urgency level of each projects and be able to manage all of them in order | I did this when managing multiple projects. I prioritized well, but it was very obvious which projects were more important. I was using my Strategic strength | | 6 | Urgency level of projects becomes clearer over time | So far I am improving, but the recent projects had very obvious urgency levels | |

## Real World Application

## Expect the Unexpected and Fail Fast

While it's important to focus on what is in front of you in the present, it is also important to consider the future. As you make progress on your current goals, and you are in a good rhythm, take a few moments occasionally to consider what goals you could set for the future. Consider upcoming events, such as job hunting or graduate school programs. What kind of skills and behaviors would you like to develop by then? It is also important to take unpredictable events into account.

One thing that is guaranteed is that some completely unexpected and uncontrollable events will happen in your life, and they could greatly impact your short- and long-term goals. Due to this, it may be worth considering strengthening your resilience and problem-solving skills/behaviors when setting goals for the future.

> *"There is no innovation and creativity without failure. Period."*
>
> —Brené Brown, *Daring Greatly: How the Courage to Be Vulnerable Transforms the Way We Live, Love, Parent, and Lead*

Remember, failure is natural and no one is perfect. View mistakes and the inability to achieve something as an opportunity to learn. After all, the only true failing is failure to try. Remember to think like a scientist, and use experiments, or constant trial-and-error. We like to use the term "fail fast/fail forward," meaning the faster you figure out what does not work, the faster you can figure out what does work. It is tough to make choices that could result in failure yet this is also how we learn. Leaders who learn that failure is a necessary part of innovation are those who exceed even their own expectations. It is important to build the skill of developing small learning experiments, conducting experiments, and evaluating your results. If you are someone who tries very hard not to fail, this is something to really examine about yourself. Ask yourself, why are you afraid of failing? Often times, this fear of failure is coupled with feeling like the people around you have unrealistic expectations. This is the time to truly evaluate who you are doing this leader development for—hopefully it is for you and not for someone else. It is important to remember that innovating is a vulnerable process and taking greater risks will result in greater rewards. Challenge yourself to fail forward and see what growth can occur.

## Innovative Leadership Reflection Questions

To help you develop your action plan, it is time to further clarify your direction using reflection questions. Questions for "What do I think/believe?" reflect your intentions. "What do I do?" questions reflect your actions. The questions "What do we believe?" reflect the culture of your organization (i.e., work, school, community), and "How do we do this?" questions reflect systems and processes for your organization. This exercise is an opportunity to practice innovative leadership by considering your vision for yourself and how it will play out in the context of your life. You will define your intentions, actions, culture, and systems in a systematic manner.

Table 7.2 contains an extensive list of questions to appeal to a broad range of readers. You will likely find a few of these questions fit your own personal situation; focus on the ones that seem most relevant. We recommend you answer one to three questions from each of the categories.

## TABLE 7.2: QUESTIONS TO GUIDE THE LEADER AND ORGANIZATION

**What do I think/ believe?**

- How do I recognize both significant progress and a need for continued change?
- What progress have I made as a leader/person?
- How do I define myself as a leader now?
- How does my belief about myself differ from how others see me?
- Am I still committed to the practices I developed?
- Am I willing to make these practices part of my life long term?
- How do I deal with unresolved issues and uncertainty as I move forward?

**What do I do?**

- What do I communicate that conveys both progress and continued urgency?
- Am I visibly doing what I have committed to doing?
- Am I living up to the standards I have set for myself?
- Am I perceived as acting with integrity with regard to meeting my commitments?
- What do I do to sustain my new practices and development?
- Do I surround myself with others who are focused on their personal changes so that I have a reinforcement system?
- Do I continue to track and measure my progress?

**What do we believe?**

- What do we believe about people who are always focused on their development?
- What do we believe about ongoing development practices versus fixing problems then moving on?
- What do we believe about how to monitor and build momentum in different areas of life?
- What do we believe about appropriate pace of, and focus on, development and growth?
- How do our beliefs about growth impact our ability to maintain momentum?
- What recognition is appropriate from different groups in my life (family, work)?

**How do we do this?**

- What are the top three new behaviors others can expect to see? How will these behaviors be measured and reinforced?
- Who will remind me I can make changes when I am struggling?
- What happens if I am not successful in meeting my top three goals? How would I like others to reinforce or support my behavioral changes?
- Do we have systems in place that discourage me from accomplishing my top three goals?
- What can I stop doing that will give me more time to practice?
- Are there any new ways to gain additional momentum to leverage existing changes and small wins?
- Am I reviewing measures regularly and recognizing results toward my development goals?

## Reflection Question Responses

Anthony, Shelby, and Kelly have each chosen one to two questions from each section of Table 7.2. Simply follow along with their answers to the questions they chose. Remember, this is your worksheet, so the questions they chose may not be the right ones for you. Select the questions that fit your current situation.

## Anthony's Responses to Reflection Questions

## What do I think/believe?

▰ *How do I deal with unresolved issues and uncertainty as I move forward?*

Having unresolved issues, or uncertainty regarding issues is a personal challenge for me. Since I strive to make sure that all of the components related to a task are completed before I move onto the next to make sure they are accomplished in sequence. Breaking a project into smaller parts allows me to deal with any challenges that may present themselves during the project process. Many group projects that I have participated in contributed to my ability to deal with unresolved issues since in group projects work tasks are split or delegated and members preform certain tasks. I often had a hard time agreeing to have an important task assigned to a group member that I knew would not put in the effort into completing it properly. One way I dealt with the uncertainty of completion was to follow up on a routine basis with each group member as to the status of their part of the project. Getting feedback on the components of a project helps troubleshoot any areas that may need more attention to complete. Uncertainty is often caused by a lack of information. Therefore, constant communication as to the status of issues is helpful to move forward and stay focused on the task at hand.

## What do I do?

▰ *Am I living up to the standards I have set for myself?*

I believe that I am always going to be a student in that I will strive to gain knowledge as I continue in my career and personal life. I must remain open to new information and interactions that will contribute to shaping who I am and my beliefs. I do believe that I am on the right path to being a lifelong learner. I always remember a saying that keeps me grounded in my quest for learning: "People are like trees. If you are not green and growing, you are dying." If we believe we have accomplished all that we can and are happy with that, then we stop learning. I grew up being taught that if you are going to do something, do it right, and that the harder you worked for something the more you appreciated it. I believe we should never look to accomplish only the minimum at work, school, or in life and that we should celebrate our successes and learn from our mistakes in everything that we do.

## *What do we believe?*

■ ***What do we believe about people who are always focused on their development?***

I think people, like me, who focus on their development are committed to being students of the world. They are people who are not satisfied with doing the bare minimum, and they focus on increasing knowledge. However, I think that there is a fine line between focusing so much on yourself that you cannot form meaningful, lasting relationships professionally or personally. I believe that development comes in many shapes and forms. Individuals who are narrow minded, or singularly focused on their developmental plan, may be missing a larger picture and vision for their organization. These kinds of individuals are usually not good team players in projects and may have trouble in leadership positions. Leadership is about serving those you lead and helping them to be the best they can be. Always being focused only on your development, precludes this type of person from being an effective leader

## *How do we do this?*

■ ***What are the top three new behaviors others can expect to see? How will these behaviors be measured and reinforced?***

The top three behaviors others can expect to see from me are: the ability to listen and learn from those around me and situations I am placed in; being open to new information and processes that may have been foreign to me in the past; and a willingness to help others succeed in their goals and objectives for their growth in business. I will be able to integrate information gained through my enhanced listening skills and apply it to my business practice. I will seek immediate feedback through reflective listening to make sure that I understand all that was discussed at the end of every meeting. I will outline the "next steps" needed in the process to move forward with the tasks at hand. I will be able to measure being a lifelong learner through continued education in related fields, as well as advancement in my profession related to additional knowledge attained. I will seek feedback from my mentors regarding my internalization of information and ability to perform at a high level as I gain knowledge. My behaviors geared toward serving others as a leader will be evident and measurable by the ability to incorporate team concepts in completing increasingly difficult tasks or projects. As a leader I will be measured by my ability to respectfully hold team members accountable for their roles and responsibilities while building a trusting appreciative relationship.

## Shelby's Responses to Reflection Questions

## What do I think/believe?

▰ *How does my belief about myself differ from how others see me?*

I feel that I am probably more critical of myself than others are. I tend to be self-reflective and inward thinking about all of my actions, and probably see things as a bigger deal than what others may think.

▰ *Am I willing to make these practices part of my life long-term?*

Yes! To keep my leadership development growing and changing throughout my life, I have to be willing to make changes that are long-term.

## What do I do?

▰ *Do I surround myself with others who are focused on their personal changes so that I have a reinforcement system?*

I have a very small group of people around me who are focused on personal change and personal growth. I want to keep those people close and let them know that I need them as reinforcement in my life. I will let them know that I will reciprocate with the same support.

## What do we believe?

▰ *What do we believe about people who are always focused on their development?*

To me, people who are always focused on their development are dedicated and work hard for themselves, which is a beautiful thing. However, I always hope to see people who are focused on helping others develop as well. What an amazing cycle we could create if we take and give development throughout our lives! Focus on self comes first because you need to learn how to grow and develop before you can lead and guide others through that process. After we are experts at personal development, I believe it is our responsibility to pay forward by using that skill to help others develop.

▰ *What do we believe about how to monitor and build momentum in different areas of life?*

I have always heard it takes twenty-one days to develop a new habit, or make a change in life. I definitely believe that practice—as well as recognizing and correcting mistakes—is how to monitor and build momentum to make changes in life. Monitoring forces us to be self-reflective, and to pay attention to the details in what we do and how we act. We need to be able to recognize and make in-the-moment changes. Building momentum comes from motivation and perseverance, and answering questions such as: How can I motivate myself (and others) to meet their goals? What do I need to do internally and/or externally to keep pressing on?

## How do we do this?

- ### *What can I stop doing that will give me more time to practice?*

I'm a worrier by nature. I worry and stress out about everything. I think if I can get a handle on being worried and stressed about meeting my goal and making mistakes along the way, I can have a more laser-like focus on what I am really trying to achieve. I need to defog my mind and focus on what matters most.

## Kelly's Responses to Reflection Questions

## What do I think/believe?

- ### *What progress have I made as a leader/person?*

Reviewing my student club activity history during the past four years of college, I can see that I have become more and more outgoing, and have increased the number of activities and improved them year after year. A few weeks ago I contributed an idea for new activities to advertise our club, and the whole group was very happy to accept my idea, and we successfully implemented it on campus. I was the manager and host of the whole activity. There were over forty students engaged in the event and they played games together to celebrate pre-Valentine's Day. Our club and our activity got really good responses from all international students. The following week, we held a Chinese New Year event that involved over one hundred students. From the event I planned and joined, I can see my improvement and I am moving toward the goals I set. I gained very good leadership and professional experience from being an event planner and a host.

## What do I do?

- ### *Am I visibly doing what I have committed to doing?*

Yes. Over one hundred students saw the whole progress of event planning and hosting. And my ability and performance were highly affirmed by my club members and our president. I believe my work has impressed others. We took pictures of the events. The pictures and the compliments from members always encourage me to move on because I am sure others can see what I did. I see how my strengths were utilized in planning these events and, therefore, I am feeling more confident in my natural abilities.

■ *Do I continue to track and measure my progress?*

Yes. During my internship I kept short journals to record my goals, my progress, and my weakness in work. I wrote about the journeys every week. At the end of my internship I was able to see what I did, what I learned, what I improved, and what to improve in the future. I will continue this good habit to track my progress.

## What do we believe?

■ *What do we believe about people who are always focused on their development?*

I really admire people who can always focus their effort and spend time on self-improvement, especially those who manage their time well between working hard and enjoying life. They usually are the ones who grow and improve themselves the fastest, not only because of their concentration on one thing, but also their effective time management.

■ *What do we believe about appropriate pace of, and focus on, development and growth?*

A "pace" is completely subjective, and different people move at a different pace on everything depending on their experience and nature. The most important thing, I think, is first to understand what type of person I am, then I can choose the pace at which I feel comfortable developing and growing. Finding my own pace can make me more effective because with a comfortable tempo I can focus all of my effort on something I am doing.

## How do we do this?

■ *What can I stop doing that will give me more time to practice?*

I can cut my time watching shows and other unnecessary entertainment to spend it on something meaningful. This is one of my bad habits during my college years: I spend a lot of time watching television shows, sleeping and doing nothing, and wasting so much time I could have spent on reading, studying, or more importantly experimenting. In those cases, I was not utilizing my strengths or my leadership abilities. While saving a certain amount of time for entertainment and relaxing, I need to spend more time on useful things. Otherwise, I may lose a lot of opportunities in life.

## Embed Innovation Systematically

Now that you have seen the worksheets and read through the sample narratives, it is time to complete the worksheets and answer the questions for yourself. We encourage you to complete all of the exercises and answer one to three reflection questions from each section in Table 7.2. This process serves to help you incorporate your goals and your process into your life systematically. It is easy to lose sight of goals. A great example is the New Year's resolution to exercise more. According to a Jan. 19, 2015 article in the *Wall Street Journal,* there is a spike in membership sales at gyms the first week in January, but even by the third week of January, there is already a decline in attendance by members who just signed up. By March, a significant number of those new members are no longer attending the gym at all. The goals that were very important on January 1 dwindled in priority as the demands of time and life gathered speed.

You will face the same challenges in maintaining a commitment to leadership development. How will you sustain this process? The best way to ensure your long-term commitment is to follow the steps we have outlined here. Your support system is key, your awareness of barriers is key, and your ability to cycle back and re-evaluate your goals regularly is very important. We can get so caught up in our daily tasks and responsibilities that we can forget to be responsible to ourselves. Don't let that happen. Mark your calendar to update and revisit your goals. Check in with your mentors regularly. And find a friend who can support your plan for personal development. Staying on track with your development as a leader may be the most important investment in yourself that you will ever make. You have invested so much time in this process already. To sustain and continue to build on the changes you have made, it is important for you to continually approach them with deliberation and a sense of presence.

In our dynamic school and work environments, growth and development are required to stay relevant. This is perhaps more true now than at any other time in history, when growth is now a requirement to achieve and maintain success. Leadership growth is not only a matter of conceptual and pragmatic learning, but, also, about being introspective in our relationship with ourselves and with others.

## Conclusion

Congratulations! If you started with the first step, you have finished the innovative leadership development process, and we trust you have seen a significant increase in your effectiveness as a student leader, and as a person in all areas of your life. It is time to celebrate your successes and the support you received from others! How will you acknowledge what you have accomplished? Consider reviewing your vision and SWOT analysis, and write down what you have accomplished.

How will you acknowledge the support others provided? How, in your culture, do you show gratitude and appreciation? When will you celebrate with your support team, either individually or collectively? Have you already been celebrating? Celebration is often a missed step in the leader development process. Expressing gratitude to others can actually increase your own level of happiness and satisfaction while building positive relationships with your colleagues and team members. Then, appreciating your own accomplishments actually elevates your engagement level and your growth and success as a leader. When we take the time to celebrate our accomplishments, we allow our happiness levels to rise in the present, and this increased happiness can then lead to greater motivation for the next challenge. Too many of us forget to celebrate and just move onto the next goal. You worked hard on this process, give yourself a pat on the back! Treat yourself to your favorite dinner, or go out on the town with friends. The time you invested in this process is time well spent!

## *What Is Next for You?*

Throughout this workbook, we provided a framework for developing innovative leadership to support your success. We augmented the process with a series of reflection questions and templates that can serve as guides. Based on our work with several thousands of students and clients, we offer this specific combination of tools and framework to create a comprehensive approach that will allow you, the leader, to define what you want to change and give you a road map to support your development.

We provided student stories to illustrate how to use the development process from a student leader perspective. By using the tools in the book and answering the questions about how an college student leader would engage in development, Anthony, Shelby, and Kelly shared the practical application of this theory with you.

Now that you have completed the workbook and established a solid personal development practice, it is time to think about whether you want to enhance your practice and begin the process again. Do you want to build on what you have created and revisit parts of the workbook that may be valuable at this time or maybe when you start your new job after graduation? You could start from the beginning and confirm your vision and values. Future iterations will likely take less time, as you now have experience with the development process. You may find that you focus on different areas based on your growth.

Congratulations on the progress you have made on your journey toward innovative leadership. Enjoy your success!

**What do I think/believe?**

**What do I do?**

## What do we believe?

**How do we do this?**

**How will you and your support team celebrate your success?**

# Books, Articles, and References

Bachman, Rachel. "The Week Your New Year's Resolution to Exercise Dies." *The Wall Street Journal*, Jan. 19, 2015.

Boaz, Nate and Erica Ariel Fox. *Change Leader, Change Thyself*, McKinsey Quarterly 2014.

Brown, Barrett. "Conscious Leadership for Sustainability: How Leaders with Late-Stage Action Logic Design and Engage in Sustainability Initiatives." Ph.D. diss., Fielding Graduate University, 2011.

Brown, Brené. *Daring Greatly: How the Courage to Be Vulnerable Transforms the Way We Live, Love, Parent, and Lead.* New York, NY: Gotham Books, 2012

Collins, Jim. *Good to Great: Why some Companies Make the Leap...and Others Don't.* New York: HarperCollins Publishers, Inc., 2001.

Csikszentihaly, Mihaly. *Flow: The Psychology of Optimal Experience.* New York: Harper Perennial, 1990.

Doran, George T. "There's a S.M.A.R.T. way to write management's goals and objectives." *Management Review.* November 1981.

Dugan, J. P., C. Kodama, B. Correia & Associates. *Multi-Institutional Study of Leadership insight report: Leadership program delivery.* College Park, MD: National Clearinghouse for Leadership Programs, 2013.

Fitch, Geoff, Venita Ramirez, and Terri O'Fallon. "Enacting Containers for Integral Transformative Development." Presentation: Integral Theory Conference, July 2010.

Fritz, Robert. *Path of Least Resistance: Learning to Become the Creative Force in Your Own Life.* New York: Random House, 1984.

Gauthier, Alain. "Developing Generative Change Leaders Across Sectors: An Exploration of Integral Approaches," *Integral Leadership Review*, June 2008.

Goleman, Daniel. *Emotional Intelligence.* New York: Bantam Books, 1995.

Goleman, Daniel. Working with Emotional Intelligence. New York: Bantam Books, 1998.

Goleman, Daniel, Richard E. Boyatzis, and Annie McKee. *Primal Leadership: Learning to Lead with Emotional Intelligence.* Boston: Harvard Business School Press, 2002.

Haney, Tina. "The Imposter Syndrome: Unlocking the Fear of Being Successful and Serving as a Leader." 41st Annual Meeting National Organization of Nurse Practitioner Faculties, April 2015.

Heath, Chip and Dan Heath. *Switch: How to Change Things When Change Is Hard.* New York: Broadway Books, 2010.

Heffernan, Margaret. *Willful Blindness: Why We Ignore the Obvious at Our Peril.* New York: Bloomsbury: 2011.

Hofstede, Geert. *Culture's Consequences: International Differences in Work-Related Values.* Newbury Park: Sage Publications, 1980.

Howe-Murphy, Roxanne. *Deep Coaching: Using the Enneagram as a Catalyst for Profound Change.* El Granada: Enneagram Press, 2007.

Johnson, Barry. *Polarity Management: Identifying and Managing Unsolvable Problems.* Amherst: HRD Press, 2014.

Klatt, Maryanna, Janet Buckworth, and William B. Malarkey. "Effects of Low-Dose Mindfulness-Based Stress Reduction (MBSR-ld) on Working Adults." *Health Education and Behavior* 36 (3): 601-614, 2009.

Komives, S.R., S.D. Longerbeam, J.E. Owen, F.C. Mainella, and L. Osteen. "A leadership identity development model: Applications from a grounded theory." *Journal of College Student Development*, 47(4), 401-418, 2006.

Leonard, George and Michael Murphy. *The Life We Were Given: A Long Term Program for Realizing Potential of Body, Mind, Heart and Soul.* New York: Penguin Group, 2005.

Machida, Moe and John Schaubroek. "The role of self-efficacy beliefs in leader development." *Journal of Leadership and Organizational Studies*, 18(4), 459-468, 2011.

Maddi, Salvatore R. and Deborah M. Khoshaba. *Resilience at Work: How to Succeed No Matter What Life Throws at You.* New York: AMACOM Books, 2005.

Metcalf, Maureen. "Level 5 Leadership: Leadership that Transforms Organizations and Creates Sustainable Results." *Integral Leadership Review.* March 2008.

Metcalf, Maureen, John Forman, and Dena Paluck. "Implementing Sustainable Transformation – Theory and Application." *Integral Leadership Review.* June 2008.

Musselwhite, Chris. "Self Awareness and the Effective Leader." *Inc. Magazine.* October 2007.

Northouse, Peter G. *Leadership: Theory and Practice.* Thousand Oaks: Sage Publications, 2010.

O'Fallon, Terri, Venita Ramirez, Jesse McKay, and Kari Mays. "Collective Individualism: Experiments in Second Tier Community." Presented at the Integral Theory Conference August 2008.

O'Fallon, Terri. "The Collapse of the Wilber-Combs Matrix: The Interpenetration of the State and Structure Stages." Presented at the Integral Theory Conference (1st place winner) July 2010.

O'Fallon, Terri. "Integral Leadership Development: Overview of our Leadership Development Approach." www.pacificintegral.com, 2011.

Patterson, Kerry, Joseph Grenny, Ron McMillan, and Al Switzler. *Crucial Conversations: Tools for talking when stakes are high.* New York: McGraw-Hill, 2002.

Rath, Tom and Barry Conchie. *Strengths Based leadership: Great Leaders, Teams, and Why People Follow.* New York, NY: Gallup Press, 2008.

Richmer, Hilke R. "An Analysis of the Effects of Enneagram-Based Leader Development on Self-Awareness: A Case Study at a Midwest Utility Company." Ph.D. diss., Spalding University, 2011.

Riso, Don Richard, and Russ Hudson. *The Wisdom of the Enneagram: The Complete Guide to Psychological and Spiritual Growth for the Nine Personality Types.* New York: Bantam, 1999.

Riso, Don Richard and Russ Hudson. *Personality Types: Using the Enneagram for Self-Discovery.* New York: Houghton Mifflin, 1996.

Roenigk, Alyssa. "Lotus pose on two." Retrieved from http://espn.go.com/nfl/story/_/id/9581925/ seattle-seahawks-use-unusual-techniques- practice-espn-magazine, 2013.

Rooke, Susan and William R. Torbert. "Seven Transformations of Leadership, Leaders are made, not born, and how they develop is critical for organizational change," *Harvard Business Review,* April 2005.

Rooke, Susan and William R. Torbert. "Organizational Transformation as a Function of CEOs' Developmental Stage." *Organization Development Journal* 16 (1): 11-28, 1998.

Shankman, Marcy Levy, Scott J. Allen, and Paige Haber-Curran. *Emotionally Intelligent Leadership: A Guide for Students.* 2nd ed. San Francisco: Jossey-Bass, 2015.

Torbert, William R. and Associates. *Action Inquiry: The Secret of Timely and Transforming Leadership.* San Francisco: Berrett-Koehler Publishing, Inc., 2004.

Senge, Peter, Art Kleiner, Charlotte Roberts, Richard Ross, and Bryan Smith. *The Fifth Discipline Fieldbook: Strategies and Tools for Building a Learning Organization.* New York: Doubleday, 1994.

Terrell, Steve. "Learn from Experience." *Leadership Excellence,* June 2013.

Terrell, Steve. "Learning Mindset: Developing Leaders through Experience." www.trainingmag.com. March 2014.

Toegel, Ginka and Jean-Louis Barsoux. "How to Become a Better Leader," *MIT Slone Management Review,* March 2012

Wigglesworth, Cindy. "Why Spiritual Intelligence Is Essential to Mature Leadership," *Integral Leadership Review,* August 2006.

Wilber, Ken. "Introduction to Integral Theory and Practice: IOS Basic and AQAL Map." www.integralnaked.org. 2003.

Zander, Benjamin and Rosamund Stone Zander. *The Art of Possibility: Transforming Professional and Personal Life.* Boston, Harvard Business School Press, 2000.

# Assessment Resources and Online Tools

Cook-Greuter, Susanne. "A Detailed Description of Nine Action Logics in the Leadership Development Framework Adapted from Leadership Development Theory," www.nextstepintegral.org, 2002.

Gallup StrengthsQuest assessment (specifically for college students) at http://strengthsquest.com or *Strengths-Based Leadership: Great Leaders, Teams, and Why People Follow* available at bookstores, or at strengths.gallup.com/purchase.aspx

HeartMath™ meditation practices and emWave to monitor heart activity. www.heartmath.org

Integral Transformative Practice. www.itp-international.org

Metcalf & Associates, Resilience Assessment: www.metcalf-associates.com

Metcalf & Associates, Overall Innovative Leadership Assessment: www.metcalf-associates.com

The Arlington Institute: www.arlingtoninstitute.org

Third Side Perspective Taking Exercises: www.thirdside.org/3S_Perspective_Taking_Exercise.pdf

TED Talks. www.ted.com

> Puddicombe, Andy. All It Takes Is Ten Mindful Minutes
>
> McGonigal, Jane. The Game That Can Give You Ten Extra Years of Life
>
> Heffernan, Margaret. The Dangers of "Willful Blindness"
>
> Brown, Brené. The Power of Vulnerability
>
> Johnson, Steven. Where Good Ideas Come From

# DVDs

Integral Life Practice Starter Kit Box Set – Ken Wilber

Mindfulness in Motion – A Daily Low Dose Mindfulness Practice. Maryanna Klatt, PhD

# Author Bio

### *Maureen Metcalf, MBA*

Maureen is the founder and CEO of Metcalf & Associates, Inc., a management consulting and coaching firm dedicated to helping leaders, their management teams and organizations implement the innovative leadership practices necessary to thrive in a rapidly changing environment.

Maureen is an acclaimed thought leader who developed, tested, and implemented emerging models that dramatically improve leaders and organizations success in changing times. She works with leaders to develop innovative leadership capacity and with organizations to further develop innovative leadership qualities. Maureen is at the forefront of helping organizations to explore these emerging solutions for long-term organizational sustainability. She is an adjunct lecturer at the Ohio State University, she serves on multiple boards of directors and hosts an international talk radio show focused on developing innovative leaders and thriving organizations.

As a senior manager with two "Big Four" Management consulting firms for twelve years, Maureen managed and contributed to successful completion of a wide array of projects from strategy development and organizational design for start-up companies to large system change for well-established organizations. She has worked with a number of Fortune 100 clients delivering a wide range of significant business results such as: increased profitability, cycle time reduction, increased employee engagement and effectiveness, and improved quality.

# Author Bio

## *Amy Barnes, MA, EdD*

Dr. Amy Barnes is a faculty member at the Ohio State University in the College of Education and Human Ecology, and is coordinator of undergraduate leadership and service-learning courses for the Educational Studies department. She teaches graduate and undergraduate courses in leadership development, group dynamics, case analysis, and intercultural leadership. Her research and teaching interests include critical pedagogy, the intersection of social justice and leadership education, positive psychology, and intercultural leadership. She received her doctorate and her undergraduate degree from the College of William and Mary in Virginia and her master's degree from Ohio State.

# *Thank you for reading!*

Thank you for taking the time to read the *Innovative Leadership Workbook for College Students*.

I trust the worksheets and reflection questions you completed here will help you become a more effective leader. Because growth has a ripple effect dynamic, we welcome your suggestions, additional tools and templates. Please contact me at:

Maureen Metcalf
Metcalf & Associates, Inc.
Maureen@metcalf-associates.com

This is the ninth in a series of workbooks. Download other titles on Innovative Leadership at www.innovativeleadershipfieldbook.com

www.ingramcontent.com/pod-product-compliance
Lightning Source LLC
Chambersburg PA
CBHW061813210326
41599CB00034B/6988